A Brit Different

A GUIDE TO THE ECCENTRIC EVENTS AND CURIOUS CONTESTS OF BRITAIN

Emma Wood and Keith Didcock

A Brit Different

First published in the United Kingdom in 2010 by

Punk Publishing Ltd

3 The Yard
Pegasus Place
London
SE11 5SD

www.punkpublishing.co.uk

A catalogue record of this book is available from the British Library.

ISBN: 978-1-906889-07-4

10 9 8 7 6 5 4 3 2 1

Contents

Introduction

Every country has its curiosities and quirks. Scratch the surface and underneath you're likely to find folk all over the world up to all sorts of weird activities. The origins of these activities are often obscure, but that just adds to their charm. Maybe they mark a seasonal change or commemorate local customs, maybe they're just communal gatherings or a chance to blow off steam. Whatever the truth about them, they happen everywhere. They're part of the fabric of human life.

So, there's nothing uniquely eccentric about the British. Our own dazzling array of comic competitions and bogus championships doesn't mark us out as circus animals. What we do have, though, is a remarkable capacity to embrace the madness. Should you choose to dedicate a year of your life to your competitive instincts, you could race in wheelbarrows, lawnmowers, prams and tin baths. You could wrestle in gravy or eat onions, nettles and mince pies. You could throw black puddings, chase cheese, play Pooh Sticks, charm worms, kick shins, shoot peas or snorkel in a Welsh peat bog. And that's not even the half of it.

So, what do all the events in this book have in common? They're all fixtures in the British sporting year, alongside your plain vanilla events like the FA Cup, Ascot and Wimbledon. But unlike those sports, with their slinky millionaire players and sponsored kit, these events are designed for the average body of your average modern Briton – in baggy shorts with thin white legs, a bit flabby round the middle, a bit short of breath and usually gasping for a beer.

They're simple folk events, mainly community-based, taking place in villages and small towns, but welcoming all-comers. They seem to reflect a desire for nostalgia, to celebrate the past in the form of summer fêtes, market fairs and quirky local customs. While some of the events here date back centuries, quite a few of them had actually lapsed or fallen out of favour, only to be revived in the 1960s and 1970s. Perhaps it was a hippy thing, perhaps it's just that while some times spawn the new and avant-garde (the roaring twenties, the Cool Britannia era of the 1990s), at other times all we want is to dress in silly costumes and wallow in the past.

Most of all, though, the events of the eccentric British sporting year are fun. Sure, there are 'world championships' at stake, some more serious than others, but most of the Tom, Dick and Harriet competitors at these things are just out to enjoy themselves, have a laugh and, more often than not, raise a few quid for charity too.

Now we all know King Harold got an arrow in the eye at the Battle of Hastings in 1066 and there's always the danger, when there's some rough and tumble, that things can end in tears. So three cheers for all the volunteers and medical staff, particularly the sterling officers of the St John's Ambulance, who patch and mend the walking wounded. Hats off, too, to the legions of organisers and helpers who put on the events, marshal the crowds and fill in all the insurance and indemnity forms you need these days when more than three people gather in a crowd. Without their willingness to organise we'd all still be in the pub playing skittles and betting on the gee-gees.

The final word has to go to all the participants in the 50 baffling, mad and downright scary events that make up this particular British sporting year. Your willingness to muck in and make proper charlies of yourselves keeps this country a sunnier place. So don your goggles, jump into your wellies and the last one in's a sissy.

A Note on Weights and Measures

Britain first defined the system of weights and measures usually referred to as imperial in 1824, but since the Units of Measurement Regulations in 1995 the country has been officially metric. Even so, beer must still be sold in pints and road signs must still be in yards and miles, so it can be a bit confusing, especially to our continental cousins, who'll drive kilometres for 33 centilitres of beer.

Throughout this book you'll find weights and distances given in both metric and imperial measurements. We decided not to convert them all into one bland metric standard, but to leave them as the organisers and participants of the events know them.

So, for those with calculators and a head for numbers, here's a run-down on conversions:

Distance

The British yard was first codified by Edward I in 1305 (the standard length can be seen on the wall of the Royal Observatory in Greenwich). A metre, on the other hand, was calculated by the French Academy of Sciences in 1791 as one 10,000,000th of the distance from the North Pole to the Equator. Since 1983 though, it has been calculated by the French General Conference on Weights and Measures as the distance light travels in a vacuum in one 299,792,458th of a second. Work out the difference between the two on the following basis: 1 metre is 1.09 yards and 1 mile is 1,760 yards (about 15 minutes' walk in sensible shoes) or 1.61 kilometres.

Weight

The kilogram is also a French measure and can be a slippery customer. You'd be surprised how difficult it is to measure an exact kilogram, what with ion accumulation and the instability of carbon-12 atoms, and so on. Still, since 1889 the measure has been based on the International Prototype Kilogram, a cylinder of 90 per cent platinum and 10 per cent iridium. It's almost, but not quite, the weight of a litre of water. Anyway, there are 2.20 imperial pounds in a kilogram or 453.59 grams to a pound, and a hundredweight (cwt) is 112 pounds or 50.80 kilograms.

And if you're not clear after all that, here's a conversion chart to lend a hand:

DISTANCE	
0.39 inches	1 centimetre
1 inch	2.54 centimetres
39.37 inches	1 metre
12 inches	1 foot
1 foot	0.31 metre
3 feet	1 yard
1 yard	0.91 metre
1.09 yards	1 metre
220 yards	1 furlong
5280 feet	1 mile

DISTANCE	
1 mile	1.61 kilometres
0.62 mile	1 kilometre

WEIGHT	
1 pound	16 ounces
1 pound	453.59 grams
2.20 pounds	1 kilogram
112 pounds	1 hundredweight (cwt)
1 hundredweight (cwt)	50.80 kilograms
2,000 pounds	1 ton

SHETLAND
ISLANDS

SCOTLAND

NORTHERN
IRELAND

38

16

ENGLAND

33

37

7

17

49 27

13

WALES

44 2

6 39

18

23

21

41

1

20 31

36

11

32

25

9

10

4

8

47 35 45 50

46 28

48

12 22

43

3 5

26

40

14

24 34

30

42

29

SEASON

	SPRING
	SUMMER
	AUTUMN
	WINTER

CHANNEL ISLANDS

19

Championship Locator

Spring

Olney
Pancake Race

Thought to have begun in 1445 when a townswoman was late for church and rushed from the house still clutching her frying pan, the Olney Pancake Race, on Shrove Tuesday, is a genuine relic of the Middle Ages. There's no finer way to celebrate eggs, milk and flour.

It all begins with a pancake. Nowadays it's something of a treat, to be enjoyed with maple syrup or lemon juice and sugar, but the pancake started out in life as peasant food. Back in the days before out-of-town supermarkets, celebrity chefs and plentiful resources, there

wasn't much food to go around, so pancakes were an imaginative way of making a single egg, a little milk and a handful of flour feed a family of four.

Legend has it that pancakes became traditional fare on Shrove Tuesday in order to use up the last of the eggs because they were – officially at least – prohibited during the 40 days of Lent. And it's probably for the same reason that eggs became associated with Easter; it was simply that folk had missed them for 40 days and made a big hoo-ha of being allowed to eat them again.

Here at Olney the church bells ring on Shrove Tuesday to signal the beginning of the pancake race. Supposedly first run in 1445, the race has lapsed from time to time (most recently during the Second World War) but has been running continuously in its present guise since 1948.

❝ HOWEVER MUCH YOU LIKE RUNNING AROUND WITH A FRYING PAN IN YOUR HAND, THE RACE IS ONLY OPEN TO THE WOMEN OF OLNEY... ❞

Competitors dressed in traditional garb of headscarf, skirt and apron have to bring a pancake they've made themselves and show their skill by tossing it in the pan before the churchwarden starts the race. The ladies then sprint, as fast as decorum will allow, along the 415-yard course through the town, from the Market Place to the parish church. At the finish line there's the final flourish of another flip and the winner is greeted by the church verger with the traditional kiss of peace.

The Olney Pancake Race takes place just before the annual church Shriving service (in which people 'shrive' or divest themselves of their sins prior to Lent). And the pancake ladies, leaving their pans at the church door, are given pride of place in pews reserved for them at the front, while John Newton and William Cowper's famous traditional Olney Hymns are sung.

ENTRY
Free, but only open to female residents (for at least 3 months) of Olney, over age 18. Racers must raise sponsorship money. Entry forms available from Nat West bank prior to event.

PRIZES
A cheque to the runner who raises the most money, to add to their sponsorship.

FURTHER INFO
Race starts at 11:55am with family entertainment from 10:30am. Local council: 01234 711392; www.olneyonline.com.

Unfortunately, there are strict rules about eligibility. However much you like running around with a frying pan in your hand, the race is only open to the women of Olney, who must be over 18 years-old and residents of the town. If you don't fall within those categories it's spectating only.

One modern twist these days is the simultaneous running of a mirror event in Kansas. Inspired by the Olney race, these American kinswomen run a similar 415-yard course through the town of Liberal, before a quick transatlantic phone call establishes which lady has the fastest time. This couldn't happen in 1445, of course, because the telephone hadn't been invented. Neither had America. But what better way to celebrate the very 'special relationship' between our two countries than by frying some egg, milk and flour and running through the town before church?

Atherstone Shrovetide (Mob) Football

WHO?
Not David Beckham, that's for sure.

WHEN?
Shrove Tuesday.

WHERE?
Outside Barclays bank, Long Street, Atherstone, Warwickshire.

The Atherstone Shrovetide Football game is one of a number of traditional mob football matches that are the Neanderthal cousins of modern soccer. Businesses close and shops are boarded up as the players battle it out for two hours for a pop at the title.

It's often been said that football's a game for gentlemen played by ruffians and rugby's a game for ruffians played by gentlemen. But in old-style town football it was ruffians all the way.

These riotous affairs between neighbouring towns took place on Shrove Tuesday and were

known as Shrovetide football or, more commonly, as mob football. The emergence of soccer as a Shrovetide activity may have been for the menfolk to let off steam before the abstemious days of Lent, when true believers were supposed to deny themselves all kinds of pleasures.

Back in the old days, town football games were such drunken and violent affairs that they were regularly banned. Almost every British monarch, from English Edward III and Scottish James I in the 14th century, to Henry VIII (no mean footballer himself) and Elizabeth I in the 16th century, tried to have the game prohibited.

Of course, in those days the players weren't exactly David Beckham. Teams were made up of blacksmiths, brewers, farmhands and the like, and the idea was simply to manhandle the ball from one end of town

to the other to score a goal. There were no goalposts, no official teams and precious little guidance from the rulebook as to what was fair game. So the match was more like the kind of mass brawl you'd expect when a Wormwood Scrubs XI play the prison wardens than the beautiful game of today played by poster boys with top-up tans and Ferraris in the car park.

The Atherstone Shrovetide (Mob) Football game is thought to have been held annually since the reign of King John in the 12th century, when tanning was what you did to horsehide. Other examples that have survived through the ages include the Royal Shrovetide match in Ashbourne in Derbyshire; the Ba Game in Kirkwall on the Orkney Islands, which takes place over Christmas and New Year; and the Easter time Uppies and Downies Game in Workington on the Cumbrian

LONG STREET

❝ THE PRIZE FOR THE WINNERS IS THAT TRADITIONAL BRITISH COMBO OF BRAGGING RIGHTS AND BEER. ❞

The Low Down

ENTRY
It's a free-for-all. Anyone can join in on the day.

PRIZES
The winner keeps the ball, which is specially made each year by Gilbert of Rugby.

FURTHER INFO
The 'game' starts at 3pm when the ball is thrown from the window of Barclays bank, and lasts until 5pm. You are advised not to park anywhere near the centre of town. Tourist Info: 01827 712395 or 01827 712034. Organisers: www.atherstoneballgame.co.uk.

coast, in which the Uppies are supposed to be the posh folk from the upper part of town and the Downies are from the old fishing port.

No such class connotations exist at the Atherstone game. It's a free-for-all that begins at 3pm, when coins and sweets are thrown to the kids from a window, before a specially made 27-inch-diameter ball weighing 4 pounds is dropped into the main street. The match tends to start fairly gently with things only really hotting up in the final half hour when the rules, such as they are, allow teams to deflate or hide the ball. Because when the final klaxon sounds, whichever 'team' has possession of the ball is declared the winner. So you could be a 90th minute super-sub and save yourself two hours of bother.

The prize for the winners is that traditional British combo of bragging rights and beer.

Wife Carrying Races

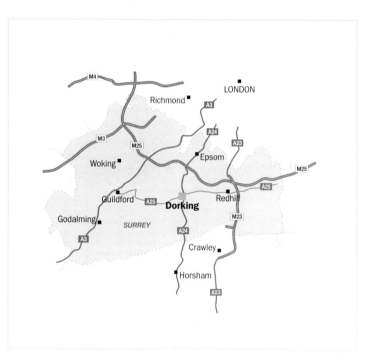

That burden on your back? Yep, that'll be the wife. The ultimate in his 'n' hers events, wife carrying originated in Finland more as a means of kidnapping a fiancée than carrying a wife. Now it's a test of togetherness and teamwork that can stretch the bonds of any marriage.

It's one of those funny national quirks that Finland is the spiritual home of wife carrying (or *eukonkanto*, as they say there). They're mad for it. One of the myths as to the sport's origins is that Finnish men used to steal nubile womenfolk from neighbouring villages and needed

to make a fast getaway with their prizes. So they would sling the young lady in question over their shoulders and make off through the forest. It sounds suspiciously like kidnap, but whatever the origins, all the greats in the illustrious history of wife carrying have been Finns, and there

seems to be no end in sight to their dominance of the sport.

However, in true gritty British fashion, we're now giving it a go. Of course, in this country the woman involved doesn't have to be your wife – in fact she can even do the carrying – which is a sign of the times, perhaps. Sham

marriages, civil partnerships... anything goes. And for those who like the idea of Brits always being eager but hopeless losers, the good news is that this is one contest in which you can never say 'May the best man win'.

Whichever way around you do the carrying, though, technique is the

key. Of course, it all depends on the size and shape of the, erm, burden. They might sound like positions from the *Kama Sutra*, but the transverse fireman's lift and the plain vanilla piggyback are popular choices. The best technique, though, is the Estonian carry. It's a kind of upside-down piggyback, with the wife's legs over her hubby's shoulders and her head with a bird's eye view of his straining buttocks. No sniggering at the back. If properly executed, it's the most ergonomic technique. If improperly executed, the bride gets dropped on her head and can legally sue her hubby for divorce with one of the no-win-no-fee lawyers who are rumoured to loiter incognito in the crowd. There are also time penalties to consider, though an angry wife with a sore head is likely to be a much more immediate concern to a hapless and butter-fingered husband.

❝ ...SURE TO SEPARATE THE BEST MEN FROM THE CHOIRBOYS AND THE BRIDES FROM THE BRIDESMAIDS. ❞

The Low Down

ENTRY
'Wife carrier' and 'wife' (over 18) can be male or female and don't actually need to be married. Entry is £10 on the day.

PRIZES
The winning couple receives a barrel, while all entrants receive a pack, of beer from the Pilgrim Brewery, and the losing couple receives a ceremonial Pot Noodle and dog food.

FURTHER INFO
The race starts at 10:30am. Organisers: 01372 840969; www.trionium.com/wife.

The classic Finnish races and numerous similar contests around the world are more like obstacle courses, involving water jumps and so on, but here it's a straight race over an energy-sapping 400-metre course, which includes about 10 metres of ascent and descent. That's sure to separate the best men from the choirboys and the brides from the bridesmaids. The winners' prize used to be their combined weight in beer from the Pilgrim Brewery in Reigate, so there was some incentive to pick a beefy bride, but these days you're guaranteed a barrel, so a lighter load is best.

Once she's on board it's a straight race up the hill, and to the winner, the spoils. Or at least the beer. She gets a free ride on her husband's back, but then what's new? The only thing worse would be mother-in-law carrying races, and you try persuading anyone to give *that* a go.

World Pooh Sticks Championships

WHO?
Little and large fans of
AA Milne.

WHEN?
The last Sunday in March.

WHERE?
Days Lock, Little Wittenham,
nr Abingdon, Oxfordshire.

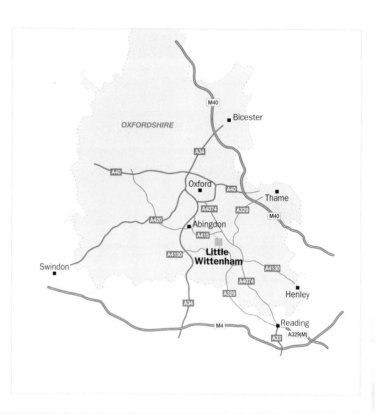

Dropping sticks off a bridge. Brilliant. One of the simpler events in the wacky calendar, this quintessentially pointless pastime is a kiddies' favourite that affords parents the ideal cover for revisiting their long lost childhoods. Be warned though: the event can get pretty competitive and often ends in tears.

It's a comforting thought that in the era of PlayStations, Bebo and ASBOs kids can still be entertained by throwing sticks off a bridge. If only everything in life were this simple: if you could solve the world's problems by telling everyone your daddy's a policeman, or win arguments with

politicians by shouting 'Liar, liar, pants on fire', we'd all be in bed by 10pm and would never have to carry money, or go to work, or cook, or clean, or…

Anyway, back to the real world. The object of Pooh Sticks, if you don't remember from reading *Winnie the Pooh* as a kid, is

very simple. Contestants line up and drop sticks off one side of a bridge into a river, and then run over to the other side to see whose stick emerges first. There are no hidden levels to this thing: it's essentially a stick race. We'll skirt over the fact that in the book it's actually fir cones that

Pooh drops. Maybe it's just that Pooh Cones conjures a wholly different image in the mind. So let's stick with sticks.

As with all such contests, tactics, practice and a bit of skill all come together with a smidgen of technique. You hold the stick out at arm's length while the

starter makes sure they're all level before giving the cue to drop. Eeyore suggested twisting the stick a bit when you let it go, but didn't let on why this helps. Some contestants throw them, some just let them drop. You're not really supposed to direct it towards the fastest flowing water, but obviously it's helpful. Theoretically, the judges are on the lookout for such obvious means of cheating, but good luck to the supervisor who tries to pull up a three-year-old in a Pooh Bear outfit for incorrect stick release.

Though considered one of those quintessentially English pastimes, like listening to *The Archers* omnibus while preparing the Sunday roast, this event attracts competitors from all over the world. The only Archer these people have ever heard of is Lord Jeffrey of trash fiction fame. In recent years, though, folk from the Czech Republic and

The Low Down

ENTRY
Open to all – tickets can either be pre-ordered online, or bought on the day. Individual tickets £2, family ticket £6, team ticket £10.

PRIZES
Winnie-the-Pooh teddy bear.

FURTHER INFO
Team races start at 11am, individual and family races start at midday. Plenty of additional entertainment for the family. Parking along the road from Long Wittenham; it can be a long walk to the event. Organisers: www.pooh-sticks.com.

Japan have won, and the worry is that these semi-pros are coming armed with detailed Google Map surveillance of the stream, and scientific reports on the dynamics of the water flow to ensure they drop their sticks into the fastest part of the stream. It's not at all in the spirit of plucky British amateurism, where winning is somewhat frowned upon, particularly if you're an adult.

Sadly, the venue for the world championships is not the bridge over the River Medway in Ashdown Forest that featured in the original stories. That's near Upper Hartfield in Sussex, and the World Pooh Stick Championships are held in Oxfordshire, which is a pity for the purists. But it's something they have to come to terms with. After all, in the final analysis, it's all just water under the bridge. And a few sticks.

World Marbles Championships

WHO?
People who've never grown up.

WHEN?
Good Friday.

WHERE?
The Greyhound pub, Tinsley Green, Crawley, West Sussex.

THE ENGLISH CHANNEL

Forget the game you played in the school playground, this is serious and requires real balls. Proper marbles for proper sports fans, played in a real pub car park. In a word? Marble-ous.

The British Marbles Board of Control sounds like some arcane government department from the 1970s, run by Tony Benn as minister responsible for the Cabinet's collective marbles. They were in short supply then.

However, the upstanding members of the BMBC actually

oversee the British and World Marbles Championships, held annually on Good Friday at the Greyhound pub in Crawley. It's a far cry from the old playground game of marbles you might have played at school, which was like miniature crown green bowls, but on concrete.

This is a knockout competition for teams of six players battling for the title of World Champions, with other contests for the Golden Oldies, Best Lady Player and individual titles. There's even the Stan Larbey Memorial Trophy for players who haven't won a single game: all the

hopeless losers go into a hat and whoever is lucky or unlucky enough to have their name picked out gets it engraved, for all eternity, on the trophy kept in the Greyhound's public bar. It says a lot that the most hopeless are better remembered than the winners. It's known as Eddie

the Eagle syndrome, after Eddie Edwards, the sublimely crap British ski jumper who managed to capture British hearts because it's the taking part that counts.

The object of the game is to knock 25 of 49 red target marbles out of the playing arena (a 6-feet-diameter ring in the pub car park). Each contest begins in the traditional, if bizarre, manner of the nose drop. Each player holds a marble of his or her choice under their nostrils and begins the game by dropping it on to the playing surface. Whoever's marble lands closest to a line in the sand gets to start first.

Everything is taken pretty seriously and, like all good minority sports, marbles has developed its own special vocabulary, which sounds pretty weird to the uninitiated, but makes perfect sense to aficionados. Don't even think about turning up to compete at

ENTRY
Anyone can enter, either prior to the event online or on the day. Team entry is £24.

PRIZES
Winners of the main team tournament are presented with a cup (which stays at the pub) and individual trophies. Runners-up are awarded beer. Trophies and beer also awarded for other titles.

FURTHER INFO
Play starts at 10:30am and carries on until the games are finished. Organisers: 01403 730602; www.britishmarbles.org.uk.

the world championships if you haven't got the lingo off pat.

So, what's it all about? Suffice to say that knuckling down is compulsory, thumbing the tolley is a definite requirement, but don't get caught fudging or cabbaging as both are against the rules. It's all pretty self-explanatory really.

There's nothing in the rules about this, but points really ought to be deducted from any contestant making jokes about losing their marbles, because that stopped being funny a long time ago.

Brits aren't the only ones who're good with tiny balls though. In recent years, when they haven't

been busy winning penalty shoot-outs, Germans have had a good run with their trademark efficiency at thumbing and special Bavarian nose drop. Thankfully, though, the pride of British marbling has been restored so that once again we can claim to be the champs of the little glass ball games.

Bottle Kicking and Hare Pie Scramble

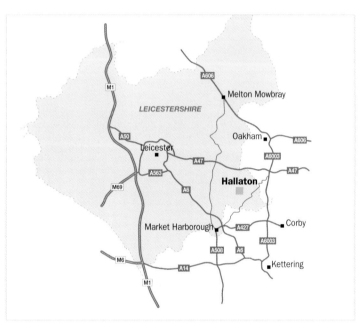

Here you'll find two wacky events for the price of one in a contest dating back centuries. The bottle kicking is actually a traditional mob football game that gets pretty rowdy and lasts for hours. The hare pie scramble is a bunch of people fighting over bits of a pie. It's all a bit odd and, as usual, involves lots of beer.

The origins of this Leicestershire double-header are lost in the fumes of too much beer.

It seems that the Hare Pie Scramble dates back to the late 18th century, when the rector of Hallaton would provide some hare pies, loaves of bread and a quantity of ale to be 'scrambled'

for in public. This involved the pie being broken into bits and thrown to a hungry crowd.

The whole affair is reputed to have begun after two ladies were accosted by a bull while crossing a field. They thought their numbers were up and had just begun some Jane Austen-style dialogue along the lines of 'Gracious heavens, Mrs Bennett! I fear we are in the soup', when a small hare ran across the bull's path and distracted it sufficiently for the ladies to scoop up their petticoats and make a dash for it. Thankful for their deliverance at the paws of the audacious hare, they donated a sum of money to the local church and decreed that every Easter the vicar would provide the villagers with a feast of penny loaves, beer and a commemorative hare pie. Now there's gratitude for you.

As unlikely as this sounds, the tradition has survived, and

nowadays involves the pie being paraded on Easter Monday from one of the village pubs, the Fox Inn, to the church, where it's cut up and thrown to the spectators. It ends up being fairly inedible, so it's a good idea to fill up on a pub lunch beforehand and not rely on the pie to feed you.

The Bottle Kicking contest confusingly involves neither bottles nor kicking. It's a beery version of the classic village football game dating back to the Middle Ages. The Hallaton Bottle Kicking contest is a throwback to these glorious old days, though it has moved from Shrove Tuesday

to Easter Monday. Two opposing teams from Hallaton and the nearby village of Medbourne form a mass maul and attempt to manoeuvre a mini beer barrel back to their village by any means, fair or foul. The tradition may have begun when a bunch of medieval hoodies from

The Low Down

ENTRY
It's a free-for-all. Anyone can join in on the day for either team.

PRIZES
A taste of the beer (if you still want it after it has been kicked around for hours) and a taste of pie (if you still want it after the scramble).

FURTHER INFO
The Hare Pie Parade starts at the Fox Inn from midday, with the bottle kicking following at the top of Hare Pie Bank from 2:45pm. Tourist Info: 08448 885181 www.goleicestershire.com.

❝ THE ORIGINS OF THIS LEICESTERSHIRE DOUBLE-HEADER ARE LOST IN THE FUMES OF TOO MUCH BEER. ❞

Medbourne got wind of the free beer at Hallaton and tried to nick it and smuggle it back home.

The maul rolls across fields and lanes, through hedges and ditches, until one team succeeds in carrying the barrel over the stream at the entrance to its village. There are actually three barrels (one of them is a dummy with no beer in it, but it still counts as a win if you get it home) and the contest is judged on the best of three. The reward for the exhausted winning villagers is to share out the beer in the barrel, which by now is well shaken and just a touch warm.

Mind you, the game takes such a long time, often stretching well into the evening, and requires the players to take so many 'refreshment' breaks that quite a few of them have already had a skinful by the time it ends. Well, there's nothing quite like keeping the old traditions alive.

World Coal Carrying Championships

This is your chance to be King Coil Humper. Not as rude as it sounds, it's the title awarded to the winner of the World Coal Carrying Championships in Gawthorpe. Folk compete by each carrying a heavy sack of coal like an old-time collier up a 1-kilometre course; and if you don't like it you can lump it.

The little town of Ossett in the old Manor of Wakefield is mentioned in the Domesday Book – the Argos catalogue of assets William the Conqueror compiled after 1066, detailing every town, village and chicken coop in the country. Nowadays Ossett's one of those old market

towns whose centre has been pedestrianised in parquet-pattern red brick, though it does boast a Grade II-listed phone box, which is something to cling to, especially when drunk.

In contrast to the old town, 'coil humping', being Yorkshire speak for coal carrying, is a relatively

modern phenomenon. Not that colliers haven't been lugging the stuff around for centuries, but coal carrying as a contest only dates back to around the end of the *Lady Chatterley's Lover* ban and the Beatles' first LP (that's 1963 by the way, according to Philip Larkin).

Like so many of Britain's quirky contests, this one was dreamed up in the pub, as a test of fitness and machismo. The idea? To race uphill over a 1-kilometre course in the village of Gawthorpe with a sack of coal on your back. It sounds fairly straightforward, but for the men the sack of coal

‘ BEFORE YOU KNOW IT YOU END UP HUFFING AND PUFFING LIKE A BUNGED UP FURNACE AND COLLAPSING IN A PUFF OF COAL DUST SOMEWHERE BY THE SIDE OF THE ROAD. ’

WHO?
Wannabe colliers and coil humpers.

WHEN?
Easter Monday.

WHERE?
The Royal Oak pub, Owl Lane, Gawthorpe, Osset, West Yorkshire.

weighs 50 kilograms (that's one cwt, or hundredweight, in the imperial measurements used in the 1960s). There's also a shorter kiddies' race, but with 10-kilogram sacks of polystyrene coal, so there's no danger of them putting their little backs out. And then there's the ladies' race.

With 20-kilogram sacks on their backs, Osset's ladies vie for the title of Queen Humper, which isn't something you'd want to stick.

The technique is fairly standard. It begins with the sacks being hoisted on to the competitors' shoulders from the back of a coal lorry that's parked by the

Royal Oak pub (known locally as the Barracks). Once they've got themselves comfy, it's time to go. You can't afford to set off too quickly because it's a real test of strength and endurance; quite a few competitors peak too soon then fail to make the finish at the foot of the maypole on the

The Low Down

ENTRY
Anyone can enter on a first come first served basis prior to or on the day (maximum of 30 in each race). Different races for men, ladies, children (5–15 years) and a new youth race for 15–17-year-olds. Adult entry is £10, children's race free. Youth race fee to be decided.

PRIZES
Trophies and cash prizes.

FURTHER INFO
Registration before 11am at the Royal Oak, with races from midday. Organisers: 01924 260141; www.gawthorpemaypole.org.uk.

village green. A hundredweight of coal on your back makes your knees start to tremble, your back begin to ache, your thighs begin to burn and your shoulders start to sink. Before you know it you end up huffing and puffing like a bunged up furnace and collapsing in a puff of coal dust somewhere by the side of the road. There's many a wannabe coil humper who's come a cropper that way. So, there's an element of *The Tortoise and the Hare* about this. A slow and steady humper can often be seen overtaking a testosterone-fuelled sprinter by the time the village green's in site. A decent time for the course is around 4 minutes 30 seconds for the fittest of the men (the record stands at 4 minutes 6 seconds, and the ladies' record at 4 minutes 45). So, it's not a race for the fainthearted, but for those with hearts of oak, legs of steel and lungs free from coal dust.

The Crafty
Craft Race

WHO?
Would-be mariners.

WHEN?
May Day Bank Holiday Monday.

WHERE?
The Kennet and Avon Canal
between Hungerford and
Newbury, Berkshire.

Water, water everywhere and all on board did sink.
This 10-mile race for home-made canal craft is a test of
ingenuity, stamina and fancy dress. Teams paddle down
the Kennet and Avon Canal for charity while doing their
best to keep afloat. Not all of them succeed.

What better way to spend a May
Day Bank Holiday than with a
bit of *Wind in the Willows*-style
messing about on the water?
The Crafty Craft Race is a canal
race in home-made crafts, run by
the Newbury Round Table since
1974. The idea is to dress up
and paddle, row or somehow

propel your crafty craft along a 10-mile stretch of the Kennet and Avon Canal between Hungerford and Newbury, in the most humorous manner compatible with staying afloat.

The teams taking part are supposed to design the crafts themselves rather than use commercially available boats or canoes; the only real stipulations being that they can't use nails to hold their craft together and the only propulsion allowed is human. In addition, because the race is all in aid of a good cause and more than a little fun, each year there's a theme, such as Superheroes, World Cup teams or the Silver Screen.

So, the devilish minds of would-be mariners set to work to dream up crafts with maximum crowd appeal, but often minimal buoyancy. In recent years crafts have included a replica red double-decker bus, a floating

Robin Reliant and a team of *Wizard of Oz* characters who'd been blown by a storm from Kansas and were trying to paddle their way home. Among a host of more Heath Robinson-ish contraptions of varying degrees of sanity, there was a yellow submarine that had missed the point entirely. As soon as it hit the water it did what submarines are designed to do, and sank.

The rules state that each craft has to be large enough to carry a minimum crew of four, be robust enough to cover the 10-mile course, but also be light enough to be carried around the various locks dotted along the canal. Humping it out of the water to negotiate the canal locks can be a rude test of the craft's structural integrity and also saps the crew's strength. Bear in mind that 10 miles of paddling to pull a craft made from a couple of semi-submerged planks lashed to

...PADDLING TO PULL A CRAFT MADE FROM A COUPLE OF SEMI-SUBMERGED PLANKS LASHED TO SOME OLD WASHING-UP BOTTLES IS A PRETTY ARDUOUS ENDEAVOUR.

some old washing-up bottles is a pretty arduous endeavour.

That's why the crafts are released on to the canal between 8:30 and 10:30am, and the race doesn't officially end until 3:30pm. It can take that long for some teams to finish. There's even a special prize for the slowest craft to make it over the line before the cut-off. Other prizes include the fastest craft crewed by men, women and children, the best fancy dress in each category and a coveted prize for the best craft.

It's a tiring day for competitors (and those waiting for the last craft to finish), so it's just as well there's a funfair and fête at the finish line at Victoria Park in Newbury, so even if you've had a good dunking in the canal you can end the day with a bit of fun. The whole event is run to raise money for local causes, so even if you've ended up in the drink, at least it will do some good somewhere.

Cheese Rolling at Cooper's Hill

This has to be the most exciting and dangerous game you can play with cheese. It's fast, it's furious, and you can smell the fear, as well as the cheese, as contestants career down Cooper's Hill after 8 pounds of prime Double Gloucester.

You don't have to be mad about cheese to do this. Madness alone will do. Where some of Britain's array of quirky contests require little more than a healthy dose of eccentricity, a spirit of adventure and a bit of derring-do, this one is genuinely dangerous. Broken limbs and spinal injuries

are not uncommon. So consider yourselves warned.

What's the idea then? Entrants line up at the top of a rough and uneven hill with a 1:2 gradient (that's in the category of seriously steep, nose-bleed territory). A master of ceremonies rolls an 8-pound Double Gloucester cheese down the hill and the contestants have to charge down after it. The first to reach the bottom is the winner and gets to keep the cheese, which they can take home with them or have delivered to their hospital bed.

The grassy hill is so difficult to negotiate that gravity trumps any real technique, and it's all the cheese-chasers can do to keep vaguely upright, using their backsides as much as their legs to keep them facing the right way. Unsurprisingly there are frequent and sometimes pretty serious injuries. The St John's Ambulance crews in attendance

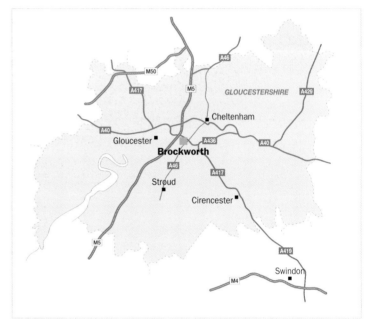

WHO?
Double Gloucester enthusiasts.

WHEN?
Whitsun Bank Holiday
(in late May).

WHERE?
Cooper's Hill, Brockworth,
Gloucestershire.

(three cheers to them and the work they do) reckons they usually treat 30 to 40 people, with injuries ranging from cuts and bruises to broken bones.

Still, this doesn't deter hopefuls entering from far and wide, including overseas, to line up on a Bank Holiday Monday and give it a go. Everyone from locals to the likes of Japanese TV stars, Belgian international footballers and Gurkhas have given it a shot and lived to tell the tale.

It's advisable to get there early if you want a good view of the event from the hill itself, because, such is the notoriety of this contest, a crowd of thousands turns up to watch the madness unfold.

Quite where the idea for the race came from is obscure. It may have originated in one of the many pagan festivals at this time of the year to greet the coming summer, it may have been some bizarre fertility rite or a ritual to

ensure a successful harvest. It may have been a joke. Whatever the reason, Cooper's Hill is now the premier cheese rolling race in Britain, if not indeed the whole world. Nowhere else are cheese enthusiasts rewarded with such tantalising glimpses of fast-moving Double Gloucesters. Nowhere else is cheese chased with such wild abandon or reckless disregard for life and limb. For these people cheese is everything and they'll do anything, however nutty, to get a piece of it. Going home cheeseless is not an option.

Naturally the joyless nannies of the Health and Safety brigade are constantly trying to ban the event because of the dangers (succeeding in 1998 and 2010), but the organisers have vowed to bounce back in 2011.

Because when an honest Briton can't chase a Double Gloucester down a steep hill on his day off, then what has the world come to?

Tetbury
Woolsack Races

WHO?
Lovers of traditional fabrics.

WHEN?
Whitsun Bank Holiday
(in late May).

WHERE?
Gumstool Hill, Tetbury,
Gloucestershire.

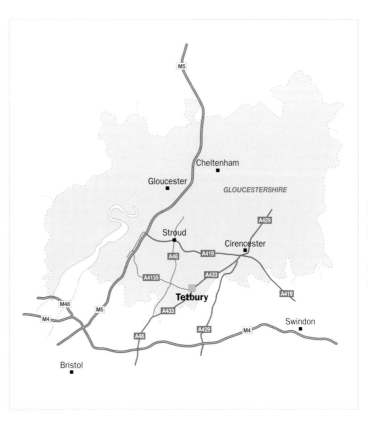

A gruelling test of stamina and the shear wool to win
(shouldn't that be sheer will to win?), the Tetbury Woolsack
Races are the best fun you can have with 60 pounds of
wool on your back and a steep hill to climb.

Another Bank Holiday, another
sack race. This time it's wool
rather than the coal burdens
at the World Coal Carrying
Championships (see p40), and
the sacks weigh in at 60 pounds
for the men and 35 pounds
for the ladies (that's roughly
25 kilograms and 15 kilograms).

So it's lighter than the coal carrying but, unlike that race, this one's run up the gruelling 1:4 gradient of Gumstool Hill. At least it's only 240 yards, though, so the pain doesn't last too long and there is, of course, alcoholic 'refreshment' available for all competitors (before the race

for fortification, afterwards for recuperation and occasionally during for inspiration).

Tetbury is one of the Cotswolds' traditional old wool-trade towns from back in the Middle Ages when this was sheep country and woolly jumpers were much sought-after Christmas gifts.

Sadly, Tetbury's days in the industry are long gone, but the woolsack race is a reminder of the town's past. Mind you, it's not all bad news because the wool market's decline was followed by the rise of brewing in the town. No surprise then that there's a pub at each end of the

race (the Royal Oak and the Crown Inn) so no one need go thirsty.

The current race began in the 1970s when medieval revival was very much in vogue, but it's more comforting to believe the old story that the event originated – as so many of them do – with a couple of drunk young drovers trying to

show off to the ladies. Let's hope they were impressed. Nothing's more irksome to a drunk young buck than performing a feat of physical prowess only to find the lady in question has shrugged and gone back to her Bacardi. Please pay attention, ladies, when the guys are trying to impress.

The first challenge at Tetbury (after that fortifying pint and a quick wink at the chicks) is to face the hill (steep), the second is to pick up the sack (heavy) and the third is to get to the top (difficult). After that it's all downhill. Actually, some of the races go both up and down the hill, which

" ...THE EVENT ORIGINATED – AS SO MANY OF THEM DO – WITH A COUPLE OF DRUNK YOUNG DROVERS TRYING TO SHOW OFF TO THE LADIES. "

might sound a bit easier, but actually descending with a heavy sack on your back isn't really any easier than going uphill and is significantly harder on the knees (look after your knees, they're the only ones you've got).

There are competitions for both individuals and teams. But if all this running around sounds too much like hard work, then there's a street fair with various stalls to distract the layabouts, as well as entertainers, and a charity auction and raffle that raise pots of cash for local causes.

But it's wool the spectators have come to see and it's wool they must have. They want to see wool carried up the hill and wool carried down the hill, and sometimes up and down until, like the Grand Old Duke of York's 10,000 men, they're neither up nor down, but in the pub having a pint and boasting to the ladies.

Shin Kicking Contest

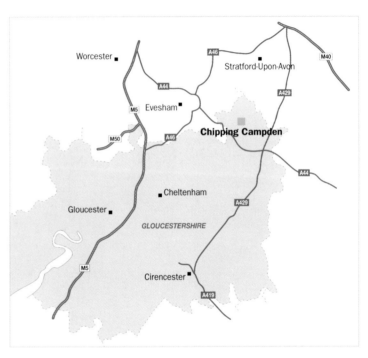

Robert Dover's olde style Cotswold Olimpicks aren't quite the real thing because there's no rhythmic gymnastics or synchronised swimming. But there is shin kicking, which is the next best thing. Why a contest between men with straw down their wellies trying to kick each other senseless has never been granted full Olympic status is a mystery.

Unlike so many of Britain's oddball contests whose origins are more modern than many choose to admit, the Cotswold Olimpicks have real pedigree. Local Chipping Campden barrister, Captain Robert Dover, initiated the event in 1612. It's a little known fact that London's

2012 Olympic Games is really the 400-year anniversary of the Dover's Hill Games. In fact, the Olympic committee originally considered a host bid by Chipping Campden, but rejected it on the grounds of inadequate aquatic facilities. And the fact that Jeremy Clarkson lives nearby.

So, instead of rhythmic gymnastics and synchronised swimming, this neck of the woods has to make do with Captain Dover's well-known countryside favourites: tug-of-war, obstacle courses and Cotswold wrestling.

But it's the shin kicking contest that has proved to be the real draw here, and which now attracts crowds of up to 4,000 people. The sport probably developed as a separate event after kicking an opponent's shins became a frequent wrestling tactic. By the 19th century, the era of bare-knuckle boxing, the shin kicking contests had become fairly brutal

and it wasn't uncommon for contestants to turn up wearing steel toecaps. Broken legs became an occupational hazard.

Thankfully, now it's a bit more Worzel Gummidge, as competitors wear nothing more threatening than boots or wellies stuffed with straw. Plus there are medics on hand should anyone have a lump kicked out of them. Of course, there are plenty of materials with more shock absorbency than straw to help soften the blows, but poly-this, poly-that and Kevlar and so on just don't have the same kind of Farmer Giles *get-orf-moi-land* feel.

Despite its fetishistic interest in the lower leg, the event is still essentially a wrestling match. The two rural gladiators grapple each other by the shoulders and attempt to throw each other to the ground. The kicking of shins is designed to disable the opponent, or at least persuade

DESPITE ITS FETISHISTIC INTEREST IN THE LOWER LEG, THE EVENT IS STILL ESSENTIALLY A WRESTLING MATCH.

them to concede. In keeping with tradition, the contestants wear white smocks and each match is overseen by a Stickler, an old-fashioned term for a judge, whose task is to verify that shins have been properly kicked.

If you're after something a little more cultured than men in wellies, try Chipping Campden itself, one of those classic Cotswolds towns that's all honeyed stone, gnarled oak and squint tiles. It had a mention in the Domesday Book in 1085, and its Woolstaplers Hall dates back to the 14th century. So, you can loiter about the town until evening, when the day's Olimpick festivities are topped off with a bonfire and firework display, followed by a torchlight parade to the town square. Here there's plenty of old-fashioned revelry, aided by the local ale, until the small hours of the morning, when the shin kickers can finally limp off home to bed.

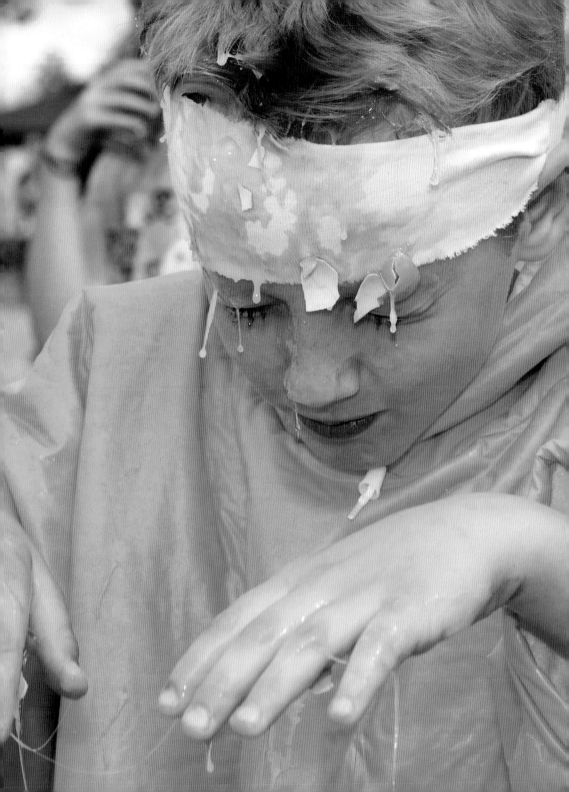

Summer

The Official World Custard Pie Championship

WHO?
Charlie Chaplin fans.

WHEN?
A Saturday at some point between May and August.

WHERE?
Coxheath Village Hall, Coxheath, Maidstone, Kent.

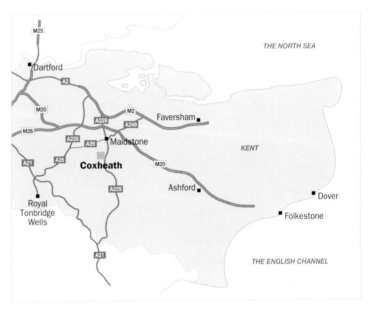

A custard pie in the face may be the second oldest gag in the book behind slipping on a banana skin, but it's still good for a laugh. And now you can do it competitively. It's known as 'flanning' and its terrace chant is along the lines of 'Who threw all the pies?'

The custard pie gag may be best known as a Charlie Chaplin routine but – pub quiz trivia buffs get ready for this – it is supposed to have been invented by a plumber from Devon. Frederick Westcott started out as a plumber's mate, but decided to quit and join the circus. He

changed his name to Fred Karno and became an impresario in London in the 1890s, where he's credited with discovering both Charlie Chaplin and Stan Laurel.

Fred Karno took his troupe of performers, including Chaplin and Laurel, to America, where his two stars jumped ship and launched their glittering film careers. Karno may have been the brains behind the pie-throwing gag, but there's a real debate about who actually *threw* the first pie in Hollywood. Was it Chaplin, Buster Keaton or Fatty Arbuckle? Frankly, who cares? The tradition behind the custard pie gag matters little in the white heat of competition at the Official World Custard Pie Championship.

The competition here involves teams of four facing off against each other, 8 feet apart, and attempting to hit their opponents with their pies. There are six points on offer for a full face

plant, three points for making contact at shoulder height or above, a point for hitting the body and a point deducted for missing with two consecutive pies (because it's a waste of good custard as much as anything else). There are also up to five points on offer from the judges for the quality, originality, humour or oddness of a team's throwing technique, and up to six points for a team's costumes.

The number of pies increases until the final face-off, in which a maximum of 10 pies can be thrown. Some simple maths would suggest that the perfect score would be 71: that's 10 full-face pies at six points each, plus another five for excellent or amusing technique and a full complement of six points for fancy dress. It's the 9-dart checkout, the 147-break, or perfect 10s on Strictly Come Dancing. Needless to say, no one's ever come close.

❝ ...WHAT YOU NEED FOR FULL COMIC EFFECT IS SOMETHING THAT STICKS AND TAKES ITS TIME TO SLIDE DOWN THE VICTIM'S CHEEKS. ❞

Sadly, these days the event doesn't use real custard. No, nothing to do with Health and Safety, but all to do with the properties of custard. It's too elastic and tends to bounce off the face, whereas what you need for full comic effect is something that sticks and takes its time to slide down the victim's cheeks. The exact recipe is a secret guarded as closely as that of Coca Cola; whatever it is, it's a good idea to wash it off while it's still wet, or it'll set like wallpaper glue and you'll be stuck with it.

But what, you might wonder, ever happened to Fred Karno?

Having gifted his best comics to Hollywood, Fred Karno returned to England and built himself a lavish houseboat, which is now – pencils ready pub quizzers – a recording studio owned by Pink Floyd's Dave Gilmour. That's got to be worth a point or two with the custard pie judges, surely.

World Toe Wrestling Championships

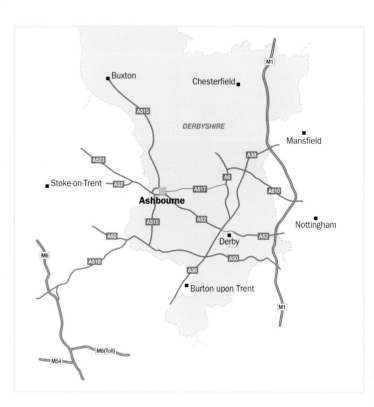

This little piggy went to market, this little piggy stayed at home, this little piggy had roast beef, this little piggy had none and this little piggy became the World Toe Wrestling Champion and went crying 'wheeee!' all the way home. Well, it'll be something to tell the grandchildren.

The World Toe Wrestling Championships started – guess where? – in a pub, of course, in Derbyshire in 1976, the year of the Montreal Olympics. A guy called George Burgess supposedly dreamt it up because he wanted Britons to be world champions at something,

no matter how odd it was. Appropriately for 1976, though, a Canadian won the inaugural event. It just goes to show that in the 1970s we Brits couldn't even invent a sport we could win at.

However, the championships proved so successful that in 1997 the World Toe Wrestling Organisation (WTWO) submitted a cheeky application for full Olympic status. Bizarrely, it was turned down. So the Derbyshire championships remain the pinnacle of the sport, the crown jewel of the toe-grappling world.

The event is pretty simple and works on the same principles as arm wrestling. The contestants lock their big toes together within a small wooden arena and, at the referee's prompt of 'toes away', attempt to wrestle the other's foot on to the wood to achieve 'toe down'. It's not as easy as it sounds because contestants have to keep their bums and their

palms flat on the ground and their non-wrestling foot off it, so it's harder to get any real leverage. Good balance is essential, as are a menacing stare, unnaturally strong leg muscles and weirdly powerful toes. Callused heels can also be an advantage, as a good technique is to keep quite a bent leg and force pressure down through the heel to gain purchase on the board and make your foot harder to turn. Other than that, it's just down to strength, stamina and sheer determination.

Thankfully, there's a nurse on hand to make sure contestants' feet are in a decent enough state to compete; after all, you don't fancy grappling with a foot full of bunions and verrucas, and there are regularly a few wannabes who fail the medical. But the foot nurse is also there to treat any injuries, of which there are always a few. With competitors such as the Toeminator, Nasty Nash and

> **GOOD BALANCE IS ESSENTIAL, AS ARE A MENACING STARE, UNNATURALLY STRONG LEG MUSCLES AND WEIRDLY POWERFUL TOES.**

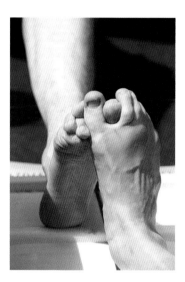

Destroyer Davies, you'll get the idea that toe wrestling can be every bit as competitive as the real thing, and broken toes are not uncommon.

Each contest comprises the best of three rounds and, given that there are left and right footers, the first bout is with the right toe, the second with the left and if it goes to the decider it's back to the right. If at any time during the contest a player wishes to concede, the correct announcement is 'toe much', at which point the victor releases the defeated and humiliated toe and starts to gloat.

And finally, the question that everyone wants to ask at events like these: does size matter? The whisper is that smaller toes, less cumbersome than the big 'uns, can be more awkward to wrestle with, but to see if that's true you'll just have to step up, dip a toe in and find out for yourself.

World Stinging Nettle Eating Championship

Just as the first cuckoo marks the beginning of spring, so the first edible nettle is a sure sign that summer has arrived in Britain. Toxic and covered in needle-like barbs, nettles make an unpleasant snack, so the World Stinging Nettle Eating Championship is something of an endurance event, but that doesn't stop folk from grasping the nettle and giving it a go.

There's just no way to justify this. Nettles are unpleasant, they sting, they leave a rash. You should really leave them alone.

So, the first question about the sport of stinging nettle eating has to be why? Why put stinging nettles in your mouth? Why chew them? Why swallow them?

Do they taste good? No. Are they nutritious? No. So why?

When mountaineer George Mallory was asked why he felt he had to climb Everest he said: 'because it's there'. World-ranked nettle eaters would say the same. Why eat stinging nettles? Because they're there. And if you're going to do it, you might as well get some recognition for it and aim high. You want to become the champ, the nettle-eater extraordinaire, the King of Sting.

So, what's the deal here? Contestants are given one hour to munch their way through as many juicy 2-feet-long stalks of stinging nettles as they can. The winner is the one who's managed to strip the greatest number of stalks and ingested the leaves.

Now, let's talk tactics. Some contestants use large quantities of beer to numb the mouth and prevent the taste from overwhelming them. Others roll

❝ YOU WANT TO BECOME THE CHAMP, THE NETTLE-EATER EXTRAORDINAIRE, THE KING OF STING. ❞

a bunch of leaves together, dunk them in beer and swallow them. One clever advantage of the latter is that your hand takes the sting rather than your more sensitive mouth. Unfortunately, one of the rules of the contest is that you're not allowed to leave the table during the contest, so if you go down the beer-drinking route you need a pretty strong bladder. Tactical vomiting is also banned, so whatever you eat you have to keep down – at least for the duration of the hour-long contest.

As well as stinging your mouth, eating nettles turns your tongue black, so it's a fairly unpleasant experience and explains why there are more spectators than contestants at the World Stinging Nettle Eating Championship, though it does attract competitors from across Europe. These hardy-mouthed souls travel to Dorset every year to take part. So if you go along and meet any of them,

The Low Down

ENTRY
Anyone over 18 can enter on the day. Entry fee approx. £5, which includes a free festival glass.

PRIZES
Trophy for the winner.

FURTHER INFO
Enter from 5:30pm. The championship starts at 6:30pm and lasts for an hour. The beer festival includes live bands and a BBQ. The pub has a campsite. Organisers: 01297 678254; http://thebottleinn.co.uk/PageNettleEating.html

do everyone a favour and ask them one simple question: why?

Nettle eating dates back to the Romans, who were partial to a leaf or two, and there's even a 6th-century recipe for nettle soup with oatmeal, known as St Columba's Broth. Boiled nettle tastes vaguely like spinach and is similarly rich in potassium and iron, and, in a neat *nouvelle cuisine* touch, nettles have even been used to make pesto. So all is not as mad as it seems. And for all their nastiness, they're also commonly used for medicinal purposes, such as treating arthritis and helping to prevent rheumatism. None of this is much consolation to the contestants, as they spend the longest hour of their lives munching through the stalks. No wonder it's more of a spectator sport. And the sting in the tale for the champion is that he or she is often too sick to enjoy their celebratory beer.

Swamp Soccer World Cup

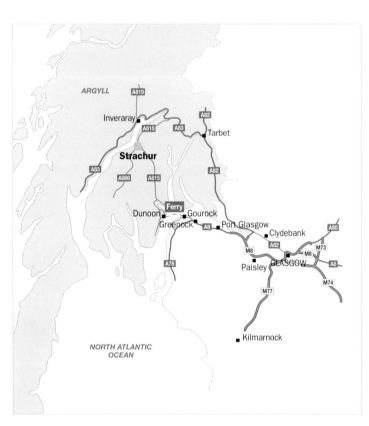

This is what football must have been like when we were still primitive creatures mucking about in the primordial soup on a Saturday afternoon. It's just mud, a ref and a ball and, this being Scotland, a plentiful dose of rain.

Swamp soccer will be familiar to anyone who remembers watching *Match of the Day* in the 1970s. Those were the days when centre forwards removed their false front teeth before the game, squeezed into shorts that were tighter than Pan's People's hotpants and faced

defenders with nicknames like Chopper. Sheepskin coats were obligatory attire, and spectators stood on uncovered terraces warming themselves with Bovril and steak and kidney pies. Out in the middle, 22 not-so-good-looking men battled it out on grassless mud patches because,

by the middle of winter, unhelpful weather had reduced even the best-kept grounds to swamps.

Bizarrely, though, Swamp Soccer is not a hymn of praise to those muddy, bloody days. The sport originated in Finland when cross-country skiers were looking for training ideas during the summer.

Now, most sensible people would run along a sandy beach in the sunshine, up and down a few dunes, and then retire for a wheat-germ protein shake and a power nap; but these chumps decided to haul their limbs through a muddy bog instead. To make it a bit more interesting,

they thought they'd have a bit of a kick-about while they were at it and lo, a sport was born.

You don't need a hatful of brains to work out what Swamp Soccer's all about. It's a six-a-side game with one goalie and five out-swampers, and the option of unlimited substitutions. Given the energy-sapping nature of the pitch that's quite a good idea, because it's really just a bog: cloying, ankle-deep and with a consistency akin to porridge and glue. You'd think the bounce of the ball would be unpredictable, but it's not because it doesn't bounce at all. So what you get with Swamp Soccer is an often hilarious spectator sport, as teams with names like Real Mudrid and, Scottish favourites, Cowdungbeath battle through those 70s-like conditions. The only difference to the real game is that there's no offside rule, which is ideal for lazy goal poachers.

THE PITCH...IT'S REALLY JUST A BOG: CLOYING, ANKLE-DEEP AND WITH A CONSISTENCY AKIN TO PORRIDGE AND GLUE.

The event even has it's own corporate sponsors, including the makers of a waterproof sock, and a total of 50-or-so teams vying for the title. The cup is run in groups leading to qualification into a knockout stage. It doesn't quite have the glitz of the real World Cup, and you won't find players taking to the pitch in styling mousse and branded boots, but still, it's taken pretty seriously. And, at the end of all the fun, instead of the communal bath there are puddles or the river to wash off the worst of the slime.

However, if Swamp Soccer isn't your thing there's plenty of other entertainment on offer, including live music, bouncy castles, bucking broncos and that funny pseudo Sumo wrestling where you dress up in a fat suit and bump into each other. Now, if you could only wedge one of them between the sticks, you'd have the ideal big fat goalie.

World Tin Bath Championships

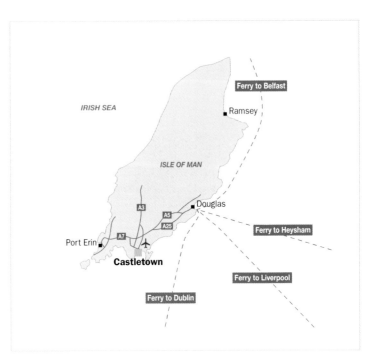

Don't be a landlubber; become a tin-tubber at the World Tin Bath Championships on the Isle of Man. All you need is a tin bath and not too many marbles in your head, and you'll be off round the harbour like Ben Ainslie.

Whatever would Captain Pugwash say about this one? 'Blistering barnacles', perhaps, 'it's a tin tub race for lolloping landlubbers', or words to that effect. Contrary to popular belief, cartoon character Captain Pugwash's barque, the *Black Pig*, was not manned by a master and seaman named

like they were extras from an x-rated film, and it was Tom the Cabin Boy, not Roger. Anyway, the good Cap'n P would surely approve of anyone taking a healthy interest in the sea.

This charitable event was the brainwave of – who else? – the Castletown Ale Drinkers' Society.

There used to be a human-powered flying contest in the harbour and the rescuers who were on hand to pluck the failed flyers from the drink used to row out in tin baths. Soon there was a rescue squad of seven tin tubs cruising the harbour, and the idea of racing them was only a couple

of pints away. They once tried racing skips, but found they left a few too many dents in expensive yachts moored in the harbour, so decided to stick with the less-damaging tin tubs instead.

Forty years on and tin tub racing is an annual fixture, with two of the original seven tubbers still

competing. With each vowing not to retire until the other one does they seem locked in a rivalry that's bound to end in tears.

Sadly, the proposal for a film version of their unlikely love-hate affair, set to be called *Tintanic*, sank without a trace. Still, it wasn't all bad news as it saved us from any more of Celine Dion's warbling ballads.

The World Tin Bath Championships are straight races around the Middle Harbour in Castletown. For the men's event there are two heats, with the top 16 tubs in each going through to paddle it out in the final. For the ladies' race there's just a straight final, which follows the same course as the men's heats: a 260-metre paddle out to the footbridge and back. Then for the men's final there are a couple of obstacles to navigate around in the middle of the harbour, and the distance increases to about 300 metres.

> ...THIS EVENT IS FAR FROM 'RUB-A-DUB-DUB, A NUTTER IN A TUB', BECAUSE IT'S HARD WORK OUT THERE, AND THE BATHS ARE DIFFICULT TO CONTROL.

The Low Down

ENTRY
Participants must be over 16 and able to swim at least 50 yards. Entry must be made prior to the event and sponsorship is required. Spectators: adult £3, child £1. All proceeds go to local charities.

PRIZES
Prizes are awarded to the winners of each category, and a trophy to the best turned out novelty bath.

FURTHER INFO
Event times depend on high tide, but are usually between 3 and 5pm. Organisers: 01624 823996; www.castletown.org.im/tinbaths.

Hence, this event is far from 'rub-a-dub-dub, a nutter in a tub', because it's hard work out there, and the baths are difficult to control. They're pretty small, ride very low in the water and, without a keel or rudder, aren't easy to manoeuvre. There's many a tubber that ends up turning turtle, as nautical types like to say (going belly-up in normal talk).

And it's no joke. The water's not exactly tropical, and trying to right a capsized bath tub and climb back in is a test of balance, ingenuity and will-power. In the event that you do capsize, you're allowed to continue in the race but not allowed to receive any help in getting going again. So there's no chance of those stirling folk from the RNLI coming to the rescue. You're on your own.

As usual, the prizes consist of trophies and booze, but the best thing for the winners is that they get to bathe in the glory.

World Worm Charming Championship

WHO?
WHO?
Fans of the creepy-crawly.

WHEN?
Last Saturday in June.

WHERE?
Willaston County Primary School
Willaston, Nantwich, Cheshire.

You'll have heard of snake charmers and horse whisperers, but worm charmers? This homage to the humble earthworm is one of Britain's weirdest world championships. Pulling wiggly creatures from the soil by fair means or foul is the name of the game, though how charmed the worms are with it all is anyone's guess.

These days everybody worries about the decline of the humble bumblebee. They're an essential element in the ecological system. But, where would we be without the equally humble worm? These little creatures may be brainless and blind, but they work wonders for the soil under our feet by

tunnelling around to provide airing and drainage for the earth, and recycling nutrients by, well, turning them into worm poo. So three cheers for the earthworm.

And what better way to celebrate its invaluable contribution to our world than to turn up in Nantwich for this annual wormy love-in.

The World Worm Charming Championship attracts celebrities and worm-watchers from all over the world. The idea is for each competitor to woo, charm, bribe, threaten or blackmail as many worms as possible out of their allotted 3 x 3-metre plot of primary school playing field.

Whoever entices out the most worms in 30 minutes is crowned World Worm Charming Champion, and there's a secondary prize for the day's heaviest worm.

The record, should anyone aspire to beat it, is over 500 worms. That incredible total was first racked up by a Mr T

❝ CALL IT WHAT YOU WILL – WORM CHARMING, GRUNTING OR FIDDLING – THE TWO SECRETS TO SUCCESSFUL WORM CHARMING ARE VIBRATION AND SOUND. ❞

Shufflebottom in 1980. It was threatened just once, by a Miss G Neville, who charmed 487 worms in 1993, until 2009 when a father and daughter Smith won with a whopping 567 worms. The record for the heaviest worm goes to the 6.6-gram leviathan unearthed by a Mr J Overstall in 1987.

Call it what you will – worm charming, grunting or fiddling – the two secrets to successful worm charming are vibration and sound. Without brains, but with enough nerve endings to know what's going on around them, worms respond to the most elementary of stimuli. Perhaps the former world-record holder's name (Mr T Shufflebottom) reveals the secret of his own special technique.

Some worm charmers come bearing pitchforks to gently vibrate the soil, some come luggin ghetto blasters with 'Good Vibrations' by the Beach Boys on

ENTRY

Anyone can enter online prior to the event (plots are limited). Plot fee £3. Admission: adult £1, child/OAP 50p. Booked plots must be claimed 10 mins before the start, or they will be re-issued.

PRIZES

Trophies are awarded to the winners of the most worms collected and the heaviest worm.

FURTHER INFO

Gates open at 1pm, worm charming commences at 2pm. Organisers: 01270 663957; www.wormcharming.com.

repeat. Some sing, some dance. Some crafty wormers have even tried serving eviction notices to those worms accused of not paying their topsoil rent. However you do it, you're not supposed to cheat, as some have done in the past, smuggling pre-charmed worms into the arena in their pockets and hats, and other places you don't want things wriggling around in.

So what, you might ask, is the point of worm charming? Aren't there better things to be doing on a warm June afternoon than sticking pitchforks into a field? Rumour has it that anglers looking for bait for their fishhooks set the whole thing off. Thankfully, the charmed worms of the World Championship aren't impaled, but gathered in a pint pot for weighing and counting and, at the end of the day, are released back into the wild, wondering, no doubt, what on earth all the fuss was about.

World Egg Throwing Championships

How do you like your eggs in the morning? These championships serve up eggs in four different and amusing ways, the highlight of which is Russian Egg Roulette. It's fun for all the family, though it's not really suitable for vegans, who may want to look away now.

The egg is one of the most versatile of foodstuffs. You can scramble, fry, boil or poach it, turn it into an omelette or a soufflé and even use it to make meringues.

Less well known are the egg's properties as a projectile, though its aerodynamic shape makes it

seem so obvious when you think about it. Here at Swaton, the egg (free-range and organic) forms the centrepiece of a variety of games in aid of charity. The World Egg Throwing Federation keeps a careful eye on proceedings to ensure that its lengthy list of rules are observed, including the ones about performance-enhancing drugs (which are not allowed) and the local Swaton Happy Jack real ale (which is recommended).

It all starts with what seems like a relatively simple throwing game. Teams of two take it in turns to throw a raw egg to their partner, 10 metres away. The partner has to catch the egg without breaking it, and after each successful airborne transfer the team has to move further apart and throw again. The team that successfully manages to keep the egg intact over the longest distance wins... wins a...well, just wins.

❝ IMAGINE ROBERT DE NIRO AND CHRISTOPHER WALKEN IN THE FAMOUS SCENE FROM *THE DEER HUNTER* – ONLY WITH EGGS. ❞

A variation on the game is the target competition, in which a thrower gets four eggs to throw at a human target, with various points awarded for strikes on specific areas of the target's body.

Then there's the Egg Trebuchet Challenge. A trebuchet, you may recall from your Ladybird book on medieval siege tactics, is a huge wooden catapult on wheels used to lob boulders or steaming pots of oil over castle walls when the defenders wouldn't open the door. Obviously, the trebuchets used here are smaller, and designed to catapult nothing more menacing than an egg. The idea is to place a team member a set distance from the trebuchet before lobbing the egg the precise distance to the catcher. Points are awarded for getting the egg on target and again, the further away the team member can move and still catch the egg unbroken, the more points are won.

The Low Down

ENTRY
Anyone can enter any game from 11am on the day, though pre-entry is best to ensure a place. All games except for target throwing free. Admission: adult £4, school-age child £2, family ticket £10.

PRIZES
Cup and medals (featuring a picture of a chicken) are awarded to the winners.

FURTHER INFO
This event is part of Swaton Vintage Day; gates open at 10am. Tourist Info: 01529 414294. Organisers: www.eggthrowing.com.

But the *pièce de résistance* of the championships is the wonderful Russian Egg Roulette competition. Imagine Robert de Niro and Christopher Walken in the famous scene from *The Deer Hunter* – only with eggs. On the table is a tray of half-a-dozen eggs. Five are hard-boiled, one is raw. Players take it in turns to select an egg and smash it against their forehead (protected by special bandanas) until one of them ends up with raw egg on their face. Okay, so it doesn't quite have the tension of a revolver with one loaded barrel, and the consequences of getting it wrong aren't terminal, but still it's a test of nerve and skill. Whether there's any way to tell the difference between a hard-boiled and a raw egg is a closely guarded secret, but one thing's for sure: the eggs are six months old, so as you can imagine, it's not pleasant when they break.

Sark Sheep Racing

The tiny island of Sark, in the Channel Islands, is the venue for an annual sheep racing event to raise money for local health services. Well, the island's so small they don't have cars there, nor racehorses, and there's not much else to do.

Sark Sheep Racing began in 1974, partly as a means of raising money for the island's medical services and partly for the heck of it. Why race horses when you have a field full of athletic sheep at your disposal?

Only constitutional historians have any real idea of the Channel

Islands' status within the British Isles. Sark, for example, is part of the Bailiwick of Guernsey, but has its own parliament called the Chief Pleas, to which 28 *Conseillers* are elected. But then it also has a *Seigneur* (lord), the owner of the island and head of the government. It's all a bit confusing, though technically (in case anyone asks you) Sark is a self-governing Crown Dependency and isn't part of the UK at all. So neither is it part of the NHS, and hence the money raised from the annual summer sheep racing event is a vital resource for the islanders' health and well-being.

Now, sheep are notoriously dim, and aren't usually much use at fundraising activities like tombola or cake baking. But threaten them with a collie and they'll run a mile. Unlike greyhounds and horses, these woolly creatures are not selectively bred racing sheep with pedigrees, and so

WHO?
Sheep, stuffed toys and ladies in outlandish hats.

WHEN?
A weekend in mid/late July.

WHERE?
Millennium Field (at the Island Hall), Sark, Channel Islands.

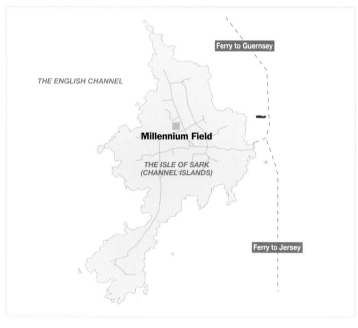

THE ENGLISH CHANNEL

Ferry to Guernsey

Millennium Field

THE ISLE OF SARK
(CHANNEL ISLANDS)

Ferry to Jersey

persuading them to race with stuffed bears and fluffy rabbits strapped to their backs like micro jockeys is no mean feat. It's all a bit daft, but good fun, and there's a healthy trade in trackside bets to add spice to the big race.

Bookies Dodgy Dave and Honest Jim (which one will you choose?)

offer odds on the sheep, which are sponsored by local businesses to carry names like Ewe & Me (a wedding company) and Ew-Nicycle (the bike-hire shop). You can always rely on a good sheep pun to raise a laugh.

The racing is spread over two days, with seven or so races

each day. Saturday is Newmarket Day, also featuring the Men's Waistcoat Competition (you can guess what that's all about), and on Sunday it's Ascot and Ladies' Day (which means outlandish hats, many of which are sheep-themed). For the kids there's a fancy dress competition and

a contest to find the Miss Sark Princess, more Little Bo Peep than Little Miss World.

Sark's only a few miles long and a mile and a half wide, so it's no surprise that there are no cars on the island, and transportation is mainly by horse-drawn carriage, which is great for any fans of 19th-century costume dramas. On the Saturday evening there's a casino night, and on Sunday a carnival cavalcade with decorated carriages and pony rides.

Something for everyone, then, apart from the racers themselves. They don't get to strut the sheepwalk in fancy dress, but instead hare around a field and over hay bales while being cheered on by an eager crowd.

The winners, at least, are awarded dinky little wooden trophies of – that's right – sheep, jumping over hay bales.

World Mountain Bike Bog Snorkelling Championships

WHO?
Mountain bikers who like it dirty.

WHEN?
A Saturday in early July.

WHERE?
Waen Rhydd peat bog, Llanwrtyd
Wells, Powys, Wales.

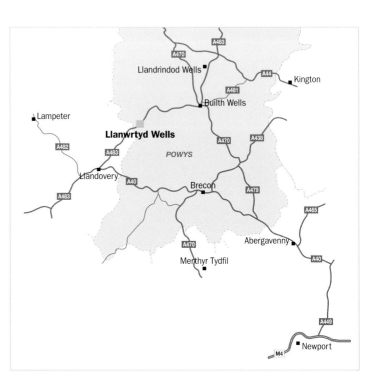

If plain vanilla bog snorkelling (see p138) isn't zany enough for you, here's the mountain bike version of the same crazy game. It's an identical principle – two lengths of a peat bog – but this time on a lead-weighted bicycle with water in the tyres. Sounds perfectly logical.

Peat bogs are cold, they're wet and they're smelly. Ordinarily, you'd avoid them. Ordinarily, you wouldn't jump on to a specially modified bicycle with lead in the frame and tyres that are full of water instead of air. Ordinarily, you wouldn't try to ride the bicycle through 6 feet

of pungent water. But then, who wants to be ordinary? Ordinary's unoriginal, safe and boring. It's dull. As Wall Street mogul Gordon Gecko might have said, ordinary's for wimps.

The World Mountain Bike Bog Snorkelling Championships are about as ordinary as crowd surfing at a church service. The bog is 45 yards long, 6-feet deep and full of water, with a pole at the far end. Contestants have to cycle up the trench, execute a turn around the pole and then return the length of the bog to the finish. Sound fairly simple? Give it a go then, hotshot.

The weighted bicycle and the water-filled tyres are to reduce the machine's buoyancy, and the riders wear a weighted backpack and a diver's belt to help keep them in the drink; but that superheavy bike and its watery tyres are a pretty difficult caboodle to ride. Add in the fact

that you're up to your snorkel in smelly bog water and can't see where on earth you're going or what the bed of the bog looks like and all of a sudden it's not nearly as simple as it sounds.

Some riders wear wetsuits to keep out the cold and keep the water scorpions at bay, and the snorkels are needed to avoid ingesting any of the foul-smelling goo that would give you at least a dicky tummy if not something worse if you ingested any of it.

Riders are timed, so speed is the key, though a steady pace in a low gear is preferable to a kamikaze gallop because the bed of the bog is quite uneven and if you hit anything solid, like a rock, you'll end up snorkel first in the dark and brown.

Astoundingly, the world record is under 60 seconds, but anything from 2 to 4 minutes is considered respectable. Frankly, you should get a medal just for completing

The Low Down

ENTRY
Anyone over 14 can enter on the day, or pre-register via the website (recommended). Under-18s must be accompanied by an adult. Entry fee £20. Small donation encouraged for parking in the farmer's field.

PRIZES
Trophies are awarded to the men's and ladies' winners.

FURTHER INFO
The event begins at 11am. Organisers: 01591 610236 (The Neuadd Arms Hotel); www.green-events.co.uk.

the course, but there's only a small trophy, handed out at arm's length to the smelly winner to go along with the prestigious title of Mountain Bike Bog Snorkelling Champion of the World. Just imagine the adulation, the knighthood and the opportunity to make millions from public appearances and TV adverts for bran cereal and drain cleaner.

However, if you feel the call of the bog but aren't much of a cyclist, then there's good news in store because just a month or so later than the mountain bike event there's the World Bog Snorkelling Championships (p138). In comparison to riding a bike through a bog, the bog standard snorkelling event may seem rather ordinary. But all things are relative and it really only seems that way. And ordinary, safe and boring though it may seem, can make a lot more sense than this.

World Pea Shooting Championships

WHO?
All those in favour of world peas.

WHEN?
The second Saturday in July.

WHERE?
The Village Green, Witcham, Cambridgeshire.

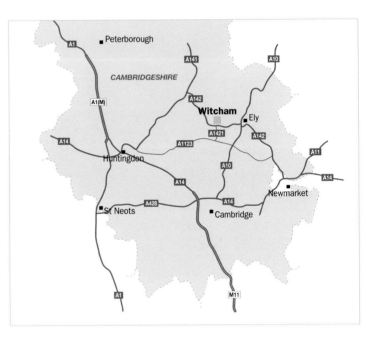

Pea shooting should be a simple sport. A pea, a shooter and a lungful of air. But, like all sports, this one has entered the age of technology, with laser-guided shooters now all the rage, and a scientific approach brought to the art of pea selection.

The Witcham Pea Shoot has been at the pinnacle of the pea shooting world since its inception in 1971 and attracts a global entry list to the annual battle for the title of World Pea Shooter of the Year.

You'd think it would be fairly straightforward. Contestants

are 12 feet away from a 12-inch-diameter putty target with scoring areas of one, three and five points and have to blow peas through a shooter that can't be more than 12 inches long. Easy-peasy; or so you might think.

However, in the era of professional sport every conceivable advantage has to be employed to the max. Swimmers exploited the supersonic suit to shave vital tenths off their times, tennis players strive for the first supersonic serve, athletes train at high altitudes and football players take diving lessons. And so, sadly, in the quiet backwaters of serious pea shooting, a row erupts over the use of – wait for it – laser-guided sighting systems attached to the pea shooter.

This is a battle between the purists and the forward thinkers. Rule 4 of the revised 2009 World Pea Shooting Championships Rules states that shooters

❝ ...GETTING A PEA CAUGHT IN THE BARREL COULD
BRING A PREMATURE END TO YOUR AFTERNOON. ❞

may be made of any material, must not exceed 12 inches in length, 'and may include sighting devices'. So, there you have it. These new-fangled devices look like props from *Doctor Who*, making simple plastic straws and wooden shooters look so old-fashioned. But many purists and sentimentalists still cling to these orginals, because when it comes to peas it's easy to get all mushy.

In order to ensure fairness, contestants must use the peas provided and shoot five peas at the target to achieve the highest possible score. The top 16 scorers in the first round go through to the five-pea knockout stages until the semi-finals, when the organisers up the ante to 10 peas per match, enough for a small stew. Not that you'd want to use these peas, as many competitors keep them in their mouths before firing so that they can maintain the same aim for each pea.

The Low Down

ENTRY
Anyone can enter the Open Championship on the day.
In addition there are ladies', children's and team competitions. Entry fee: adult £2, child £1, team (of 4 players) £6.

PRIZES
Trophies for winners and runners-up of all categories.

FURTHER INFO
Registration from midday. Play starts at 1pm. There's a practice area and plenty of other family entertainment. Organisers: www.witcham.org.uk.

Pea selection is an important skill. Your standard competition pea is dried and hard, more like a lentil, and you want a pea that's smooth and round. They're all provided by the organisers, but should be chosen with care to make sure they're the right calibre for your shooter. After all, you can't fire a .45 bullet from .22 gun, and getting a pea caught in the barrel could bring a premature end to your afternoon.

But if you do get knocked out (either of the competition or by a stray pea), there are plenty of other attractions on hand to while away the time. The village green hosts a traditional summer fête with all kinds of stalls and games, food and drink, face painting for the kids, and a bouncy castle. And in the background can be heard the pea shooters' terrace chant, their anthem. It's the Beatles singing 'Peas peas me oh yeah like I peas you'.

Three Horseshoes Wheelie Bin Race

WHO?
Bin men and beer drinkers.

WHEN?
Usually the second Saturday in July.

WHERE?
The Three Horseshoes pub, Hernhill, nr Faversham, Kent.

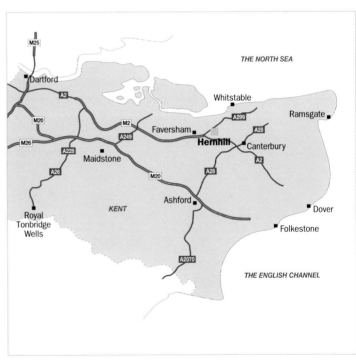

For some folk racing is in the blood and they'll jump into anything with wheels (however smelly) and see how fast they can make it go. Wheelie bin racing may be slowed down by the addition of compulsory beer drinking, but it makes this a must for anyone with a serious interest in garbage collection.

Strictly love it or strictly hate it, everyone has an opinion about *Strictly Come Dancing*. But one thing you can't dispute is its success. The mixture of glitzy ballroom dancing, sporty and soapy celebrities, a bit of reality TV and audience participation presses all the modern telly

buttons (including the red one for extra features).

Now, wheelie bin racing may seem a million miles from Brucie and Tess and their panel of dance masters, but it does pull off the same trick of combining all the elements for a great event. It's a race, which panders to the red-blooded Brit's competitive sporting syndrome. It's fancy dress, so there's an outlet for those Danny La Rue tendencies you don't like to admit to your mother. And it involves that essential lubricant without which everything in this country would just seize up: beer.

The form is that two teams of four line up Le Mans-style opposite their bins. On the off, the teams run across to the first beer stop and down half a pint of bitter or lager (depending on taste). Then one member hops into the bin and the others push it along the first stretch

of the 400-yard course. There's a second compulsory beer stop (just a half please) at midway and a third at the 400-yard point (okay, one more half but then I really must be off). The teams then turn each of their plastic chariots around and make the 400-yard dash back to the finish line. The beer stops on the return leg are not compulsory, but then (oh go on then, one for the road) the beer's free and some folk can never pass up the offer of a swift half.

Now, it's only responsible to point out that alcohol and physical exertion are not the best of friends and, although there are technically time penalties for not drinking the beer at each stop, in the interests of competitors' well-being the judges usually turn a blind eye to the more creative ways of emptying the glass.

Anyway, not everyone who takes part feels the need for speed.

ENTRY

Anyone over 16 can enter. Teams of 4 for teams running against the clock. Fun team numbers may vary. £10 per team. Pre-register with the pub. (Bins provided or you can bring your own.)

PRIZES

T-shirts are awarded to winners of each category (fastest bin, best bin and best dressed team).

FURTHER INFO

Race starts at 1pm with plenty of entertainment, including live music, from midday. Organisers: 01227 750842; www.3shoes.co.uk.

While the fastest time ever recorded is just over 2 minutes 30 seconds, which is impressive, the slowest on record is an even more impressive 1 hour 45 minutes. Now that takes some doing.

As well as the prize for the fastest bin, there are other titles awarded for the best dressed team and the fanciest bin, so teams 'pimp their rides' and create weird-looking contraptions in all manner of styles, from sleek racing cars to bath tubs and canal boats.

The organisers are at pains to point out that no wheelie bins are harmed in this event. All the racing bins are already broken, and if they didn't participate in the event they'd simply be melted down and recycled into recycling bins. So the race gives them a new lease of life and frees them from their previous existence, which, let's face it, was just rubbish anyway.

World Snail Racing Championship

Raced (if that's the tight term) over a testing 13-inch course, the World Snail Racing Championship attracts up to 300 of the world's speediest gastropod molluscs. Up for grabs are a silver tankard stuffed with lettuce and the title of Fastest Snail in the World. And you thought that snails were only good with garlic and butter.

Congham village, in Norfolk, has been home to what's probably the world's slowest and shortest form of racing for more than 25 years. The low-lying land and preponderance of ponds make it ideal snail-breeding country, and it's therefore a Mecca for snail racers and their admirers.

The race takes place on a damp tablecloth with two concentric red circles stitched on top. The snails are lined up on the inner ring facing outwards, with little race numbers stuck to their shells because, let's face it, snails look fairly similar and you'd hate to take the wrong one home.

At the traditional starting command: 'Ready...Steady... Slow!' the snails, well, they sort of take a look about, twitch their antennae a bit and then amble forward as if a tankard full of lettuce were the furthest thing from their minds (which, incidentally, are about the size

of a dried pea, and have much the same cognitive power).

Now, there's no disguising the fact that snail racing is a rather slow sport, requiring plenty of patience. To put things into perspective, you could slow down a tape of Usain Bolt running the 100 metres about a thousand

❝ AND YOU THOUGHT THAT SNAILS WERE ONLY GOOD WITH GARLIC AND BUTTER. ❞

WHO?
Mollusc maniacs.

WHEN?
The third Saturday in July.

WHERE?
The Cricket Field, Lynn Road, Congham, Norfolk.

times and he'd still be going faster than these snails.

The least slow time ever recorded over the 13-inch course was by a snail called Archie who, in 1995, managed to cross the line just a breathless couple of minutes after the starting order had startled him into a rather puzzling desire to see what was over the edge of the table. (Because they race on tabletops, snails still think the world is flat.)

Archie thought he'd go and take a look and, with a startling turn of pace over the first few inches, set off towards the table's edge. He never made it. After two minutes he was crowned World Champion, and rewarded with the tankard of lettuce, which took his mind off his flat earth theory.

Archie's other prize was his choice of the finest-looking young female snails around because, as with a champion racing horse who'd just won the Derby, Archie

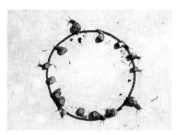

The Low Down

ENTRY
Anyone can enter on the day.
Entry fee is approximately 10p.

PRIZES
A silver tankard stuffed with
lettuce leaves is awarded to
the winning snail and its owner.

FURTHER INFO
The championship heats start at
2pm, with each winner earning
a place in the grand final, held
at about 4:30pm. The event is
part of the Congham Fête (entry
25p), which raises money for the
village church. Organisers: 01485
600650; www.snailracing.net.

was put out to stud in the hope
that he'd sire a long line of
similarly not-so-slow race winners.

The event attracts up to 300
of the world's speediest air-
breathing gastropod molluscs,
all of whom are tested for
performance-enhancing
substances before the off.

The heats take place throughout
the afternoon, with the winners of
each entered into the grand final.
The tablecloth has to be regularly
watered to maintain optimum
conditions for the snails, who
need it wet otherwise the friction
gives them a rash. And, children,
don't try to apply ointment to the

delicate parts of an angry snail
without adult supervision.

The whole event is more fun
than you might imagine, but snail
racing has a serious side too.
While the winner's prize is a lady
and lots of lettuce, what happens
to snails that don't make the
grade doesn't bear thinking about.

Pedal Car Grand Prix

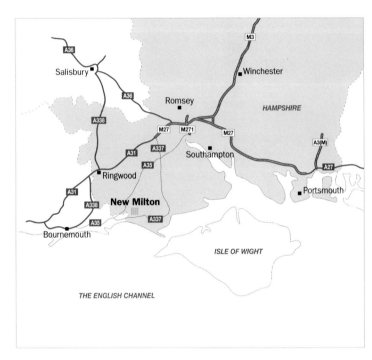

Okay, so you won't mistake New Milton for the street circuit at Monaco, but this is real city racing, just using pedal power instead of horsepower. There's still a chicane, hairpin bends, pit stops and champagne after the chequered flag. What more could you want?

The New Milton Pedal Car Grand Prix is the Monaco of pedal car racing, a not-quite-so-fast and not-quite-so-glamorous – but much more fun – version of the real Formula 1 event.

There are two contests, attracting about 40 cars in total. Things kick off with a 90-minute junior

race, followed by the 120-minute senior race. Now, two hours of racing around the 1-kilometre New Milton course is a fairly serious endeavour and, while some crews are comprised of scruffy, unshaven beer fiends out for a laugh, you'll find others comprised of hard-core ultra-competitive Lycra-clad enthusiasts – the kind of cyclists that shave their legs (though how they live their private lives is entirely up to them).

In contrast to Formula 1's rules and regulations, which require a PhD to master, the specifications for pedal car racing are somewhat looser, though it's still a bit more complicated than a case of just four wheels and two legs to power them. There are regulations governing minimum wheelbase, maximum wheel size, length and width, and so on. And there's some technical talk about axle heights and crank gears that only engineers would be interested

in. The gist of it is that most of the competing pedal cars are made from old bicycle bits welded together, some more securely than others.

Teams (of up to four drivers, one pusher and a mechanic) can get creative with the bodywork, though, and there's a definite trend towards the nostalgic. The cars often look like miniature versions of those great Bentleys and Bugattis that roared up the banking at Brooklands in the 1930s. Back in those days the cars had open cockpits and no seat belts, in the belief that if the driver crashed, it was better for him to be thrown out of the car than get mangled in the wreckage. The pedal car race is obviously a little slower and more high-oxygen than high-octane racing, so not one for petrolheads.

A team's drivers can do as many laps as they like before swapping in the pit lane. And if Martin

IT MAY NOT BE F1, BUT PEDAL CARS CAN REACH A DECENT SPEED AND IT'S POSSIBLE TO COME A CROPPER...

Brundle were talking you through a lap, he'd tell you that it's just a short drag from the starting lights down to the taxi-rank chicane. Get safely through there and it's a quick squirt on the power down the hill before hitting the brakes hard for the 180-degree south turn that leads into the back straight. The tight left-hand traffic-light turn takes drivers into the narrow and tricky Old Milton part of the course, a technical complex with a left-right flick through the layby (mind the drain covers on the exit) and the hairpin west turn, before the cars head round a 90-degree turn on to the uphill straight before the turn on to the final stretch.

It may not be F1, but pedal cars can reach a decent speed and it's possible to come a cropper if you try to take the hairpin bend too fast. Thankfully, injuries here are rare and it's only a driver's pride that's likely to get dented.

Braughing Wheelbarrow Race

Teams of two in fancy dress splash through the village ford with their specially-reared thoroughbred wheelbarrows and stop for compulsory beer (at least, the adult teams do) in this Hertfordshire take on the great British classic. What's a race without beer and cross-dressing?

The common wheelbarrow (*hyperteria monokyklou*) is a species of one-wheeled transportation devices native to Greece, though now found throughout the world. It flourishes in allotments and small suburban gardens, where its adaptive mono-wheel design

allows it superb manoeuvrability, giving it a Darwinian edge over its larger cousin, the cart. Through selective breeding, the wheelbarrow's sub-species now include wood, fibreglass, galvanised steel and UV-stabilised polyethylene pan barrows, with rubber or inflatable wheels and polygrip handles in a variety of natural and man-made materials. The wheelbarrow is the ultimate testament to human ingenuity and nature's bounty.

Here at the Hertfordshire town of Braughing (pronounced Braffing, just so you don't make a fool of yourself) wheelbarrow breeders, admirers and enthusiasts gather every year to see these startling creatures at play over two laps of the village and a quick splash through the ford.

The race dates back to the mid-1960s when it began as part of the annual village fête and was a much longer race, with

WHO?
Barrow boys and girls.

WHEN?
Evening of the third Friday in July.

WHERE?
Braughing village ford,
Hertfordshire.

compulsory cider stops at all the village pubs. Within a few years it had become the main attraction, and was cut to its current length. There's now a juniors' race too, and a younger kids' race, which is shorter and doesn't cross the river, plus there aren't any riders in the barrows (they're shy around children) and there's a prize for the best (kids') barrow in show.

The adult and junior races start at the ford, go down past the church and through the town square. Then it's along 'the street' and back to the river, where the adults head around the ford green for a second lap. The races include compulsory refreshment stops, beer (naturally) for the adult races and squash for the juniors. So, on the first lap contestants stop for one at the Axe and Compass, and for one more on the second lap at the Brown Bear.

First, though, there's the quick trip across the river. At the start

the teams of two line up in fancy dress with their thoroughbred barrow. At the off, one mounts the barrow, while the other takes the polygrip handles and propels the poor creature down into the chilly water and up the causeway on the other side, before setting off on the first lap. To add to the difficulty of being cold and wet from the initial ford plunge, contestants face a pelting of water bombs from kids along the way, before they reach the finish, in the middle of the ford.

Contestants can swap places whenever they want, but need to take care, because even barrows that are well broken in are a little unsteady at speed and can easily buck their riders. Plus, it takes a bit of puff to propel a reluctant barrow and its rider through a Hertfordshire village. But there's £100 on offer for the winner, and that's a nice little nest egg for any wheelbarrow to retire on.

BLMRA 12 Hour Lawnmowing Race

The jewel in the cheap, plastic crown of the most basic formula of motor sport, this night-time marathon event is a must for those with a need for speed, without Ferrari budgets. Just gas up your garden mower, put on a helmet and race the night away.

Petrolheads may thrill to the heavenly strum of a well-throttled V8, but for lawnmower racers there's nothing like the scream of a two-stoke sit-on mower.

If Formula 1, with its multi-million pound budgets and space-age technology, is the pinnacle of motor sport, then lawnmower

racing is the pits. Dreamed up one night in Wisborough Green's Cricketers Arms, the sport originated as an attempt to introduce a formula racing sport that would be as cheap and cheerful as possible. No sponsorship, no commercial deals, no cash prizes and, to keep costs down, racers wouldn't be allowed to modify their mowers (except for the removal of rotor blades for safety because, after all, this isn't the cutting edge of motor sport).

And so lawnmower racing was born, and with it the British Lawn Mower Racing Association. So successful was this grass-roots formula, the BLMRA now runs a series of events during the grass-cutting season, including a prestigious British Grand Prix and National and World Championships. Lawnmower racing has been adopted in the likes of France and the US, but

WHO?
Le Mans wannabes and
grass-cutting enthusiasts.

WHEN?
A weekend in late July/early
August.

WHERE?
Location changes each year.
Somewhere near Wisborough
Green, West Sussex.

THE ENGLISH CHANNEL

it's the British 12 hour endurance race that's the *crème de la crème*, the cream in a Twinky, the jam on a Devon scone, and, to give the race that authentic Le Mans feel, it starts at 8pm and runs all through the night.

The mowers are divided into four classes, starting with the standard mowers. These are straight from the garden shed with no modification other than the blade removal. Then there's Group Two, comprising the roller-driven mowers. Group Three (this is where it starts to get exciting) are the small four-wheeled garden tractors; and Group Four (hold on to your hats) are like bonsai farm tractors with headlights and a bonnet-covered engine up front, a four-speaker MP3-compatable stereo, electric windows, central locking, air-con and assisted parking. Well, almost.

There's a free practice session in the early afternoon before the

timed qualifying to determine grid positions for the start. After a drivers' briefing at 6:30pm the mowers proceed around a parade lap before the great getaway. At 8pm competitors line up opposite their mounts, waiting for the order to start their mowers. Then on they jump and off they go.

The course is a test of skill as well as endurance. Mowers need a combination of straight-line speed for the three long drags, as well as decent handling for two twisty complexes and a couple of hairpin turns. Take them too fast and you're into the hay bales or going wheels up to the sky.

Believe it or not, previous winners of the 12 Hour Lawnmowing Race include Sir Stirling Moss and Derek Bell (a five-time winner of the 24-hour Le Mans race). The late great Oliver Reed regularly used to enter a team too. So this event has a bit of genuine racing DNA to it. And Oliver Reed.

Bonsall World Championship Hen Races

So, you've been to see the Sark Sheep Racing (p90) and the World Snail Racing Championship (p106) and are looking for something a bit less woolly, a little faster and with a bit more of a flurry. Well, try the Bonsall World Championship Hen Races, where you're guaranteed a clucking good time.

These days, hen welfare is a serious issue. After years of living in cramped, ill-lit conditions, with only an endless conveyor belt of grains to eat and entertain them, it was time to rebel, so the cry went up. 'Chickens of the world, unite. You have nothing to lose but your grains.'

The hen liberation front agitated for roaming rights and corn. They wanted sunshine, fresh air and a decent diet that didn't include minced-up bits of their forefeatheredfathers. And finally, after years of oppression, struggle and being dunked in BBQ sauce, liberation is at hand.

Today, corn-fed, free-to-roam, vegetarian chickens exist in ever-increasing numbers and, while much work remains to be done, the average battery hen has, at last, gone solar powered.

And now there's a chance for chickens to really have their day in the sun at the Bonsall World Championship Hen Races. The event pits the fittest fowl on the planet against one another over a 65-feet course pegged out in the car park of the Barley Mow pub in Bonsall. Hen racing is supposedly an ancient sport that used to take place in nearby Ible. The races were reinstated in the early

❛ THE RACE CAN BE A BIT HAPHAZARD, AS THE BIRDS DON'T ALWAYS READ THE RULES BEFOREHAND AND SOMETIMES DON'T QUITE GET THE GIST OF IT. ❜

1990s by Alan Webster, former landlord of the Barley Mow, and the event raises money for the Battery Hen Welfare Trust, a charity for improving the plight of caged farm hens.

The idea of the race is so simple that even birdbrains can get it. Competitors line up with their hens at the start, both feet firmly on the starting line, then set them off. The judges are on the lookout for any sly bumping and pecking among the eager competitors, and occasionally among the hens too, and have at their disposal yellow and red cards for serious offenders.

The race can be a bit haphazard, as the birds don't always read the rules beforehand and sometimes don't quite get the gist of it. Rather than head as fast as possible to the finish line, they might strut about a bit, go for a wander, flap their wings and preen their feathers or consider that,

The Low Down

ENTRY
Anyone with a hen can enter for free on the day. A limited number of hens can be hired from a local farmer for a small fee if you don't have your own.

PRIZES
A bag of grain and trophy are awarded to the winning hen and its owner respectively.

FURTHER INFO
The heats start at 2pm, with each winner earning a place in the grand final at about 5pm. Organisers: 01629 825685; www.barleymowbonsall.co.uk.

on the whole, pecking around the ground is the best way to go. In these circumstances, after a suitable period of time, when no hen actually completes the course, the winner is the one who's at least made something of an effort towards reaching the finish line and is nearest to it.

The tension can, of course, be unbearable, made more so by the requirement for the crowd to maintain a David Attenborough-like hush while the race is on. This is less to do with awe or reverence and more so as not to panic the hens, who are otherwise liable to fly off, which

might not be such a bad idea for the birds at the end of the day.

Because, when all's said and done, the hens, well, they still go the way of most fowl and end up on plastic trays under cellophane wrappers with sell-by dates and recipe suggestions. But at least they've had a run for their money.

Air Guitar World Championships UK Final

There are a few things in life that we don't like to admit we've all done, and playing air guitar may be one of them. But you can come out of your bedroom at the Air Guitar World Championships UK Final, and join the pantheon of master axemen sawing at the air.

We've all been there: in front of the mirror with the bedroom door securely locked; with wild abandon, a flick of the fringe and a tongue curling halfway round our cheeks we've strummed and thrashed at an imaginary axe while some guitar hero blasts spiralling riffs out of the speakers.

While the lead singer's likely to get all the chicks, the ass player's broody and the rummer's as mad as a 13-amp use, it's the lead guitarist, the oloist, the master axeman who tends to get all the glory. ingering the fretboard with licks nd riffs, he's the main man, the one you want to be. Okay, there are a few prog rock guys from back in the 1970s you'd really rather avoid, but who wouldn't want to be a young Pete Townshend, a Jimmy Page, a Hendrix, a Clapton, Slash or Squire? You're bad boy and artiste all rolled into one.

So, what's the attraction of playing air guitar over the real thing? Well, it's easier to master for a start. The chords are a cinch, though you do need good hand-air co-ordination to keep in shape and not look like you're playing a seven-feet long, triple-neck banana. Plus, the insurance

WHO?
Free and airy spirits.

WHEN?
The first Friday in August.

WHERE?
The O2 Academy, N1 Centre,
Islington, London.

premiums are low. No one's ever
lost or damaged an air guitar,
and broken strings are unheard
of. And you don't get callused
fingers, either.

However, it's really the philosophy
behind air guitar that attracts
some of its most ardent followers.
Put simply, air guitar saves lives.

Air guitar promotes world peace.
Air guitar will mark the dawn of a
new age of civilisation, an end to
conflict and the final realisation
of our common humanity. Air
guitar is pure art.

Here's how it works. You abandon
yourself to the music, you divest
yourself of age, race and gender,

and enter the realm of pure
sound and movement. You hack
and saw, you pluck and twang and
you just don't give a damn. You
have 60 seconds to impress the
judges with your originality, stage
presence, charisma and technical
ability. But, above all, you need to
convince the judges that you have

The Low Down

ENTRY
Entry to venue £9. Limited places available; to be eligible to compete you must have won a regional heat or pre-registered via the website and confirmed choice of track. Must be able and available to travel to Finland for the World Championships if you win.

PRIZES
Winner awarded a trophy and a trip to Finland to represent the UK in the World Championships.

FURTHER INFO
Usually starts at 7pm. Organisers: www.airguitaruk.com.

what it takes – 'airness' – that ethereal property that resides only in true masters of this art.

In the first round you can choose your own song to strum your socks off to, but in the second the competition hots up as contestants are confronted with the same compulsory song that can be anything from Nirvana to Motörhead. With little time to prepare, airmeisters must summon a performance from deep within themselves and their reservoir of airness. If it results in a tie, then the remaining competitors have to face an air-off (think dance-off: airists play alongside one another until a winner is picked by the judges).

The prize on offer at the UK Finals is a trip to the World Championships in Oulu, Finland, spiritual home of air guitar. Here, one lucky player gets to share air and shake hair with the finest airists in the world.

Totnes
Orange Races

WHO?
Fresh-fruit lovers and
fitness freaks.

WHEN?
A Tuesday in mid/late August.

WHERE?
High Street and Fore Street,
Totnes, Devon.

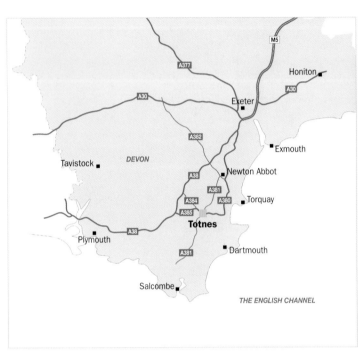

The Totnes Orange Races provide one of your five-a-day portions of fresh fruit and veg, as well as a good dose of exercise into the bargain. Race down the town's streets chasing a piece of the local greengrocer's choicest fruit and win...some fruit and a small silver trophy to keep it in.

The Orange Races, run by the Totnes Elizabethan Society, commemorate a probably spurious story that Sir Francis Drake visited the town in the 1580s and dropped a basket of oranges, which rolled down the street. Oranges, at the time, were exotic and alien to

Elizabethan townsfolk, whose idea of five-a-day portions of fresh fruit and veg didn't stretch much beyond some berries and a dock leaf or two.

Being used to long voyages at sea, though, Sir Francis knew what Vitamin C deficiency can do to the human body, and

was an early promoter of a healthy lifestyle. After all, he'd circumnavigated the globe and had first come across oranges off the coast of Brazil, when some natives and a couple of Portuguese colonists rowed out to his ship and swapped them for some linen and a comb.

So now every year the local Elizabethan Society brings good cheer and a healthier diet to the town by staging the Orange Races down the town's steep high street. It's a little like the Cooper's Hill Cheese Rolling in Gloucestershire (see p48) only instead of one big cheese for all, each competitor

has his or her own lunchbox orange to chase down the hill. The race is part of the town's annual Elizabethan celebrations, and is staged at the same time as the Elizabethan market.

To win you have to be first across the line with at least some part of your orange still in tow, or on your toe, or just splattered somewhere about you. The only rule is that you're not allowed to carry your orange. You can only kick it or throw it. So, you've either got to dribble your satsuma along the road, or stop and pick it up and throw it on ahead. The crucial point, though, and the fact that leads to all kinds of skullduggery, is that you don't have to end up with your own piece of fruit. Any orange will do. Thus the start of the race tends to be fairly chaotic, with the fastest competitors all zoning in on the orange that's furthest along the course and trying to claim it as their own.

TO WIN YOU HAVE TO BE FIRST ACROSS THE LINE WITH AT LEAST SOME PART OF YOUR ORANGE STILL IN TOW, OR ON YOUR TOE, OR JUST SPLATTERED SOMEWHERE ABOUT YOU. 〞

The lengths people will go to for a piece of fruit...

It used to be traditional for the winner to take a bite out of the victorious orange, but there's not usually enough of it left. The street ends up strewn with pips, peel, pulp and pools of spilt orange juice.

There are various races, from junior events for 4–6-year-olds, all the way to the 60-plus category. While these are both held on relatively short, flat parts of the course, those between the ages of 12 and 59 race the full long and very steep course. There's even a special Police Shield Race, in which members of the public challenge the long arm of the law. It's a chance to demonstrate community policing and stop thefts from the local greengrocer's by showing off the fitness of the average bobby on the beat. You try grabbing a satsuma and see how far you get.

Worthing International Birdman

WHO?
Anyone with personal injury insurance.

WHEN?
A weekend in June/July/August.

WHERE?
Worthing Pier, Worthing, West Sussex.

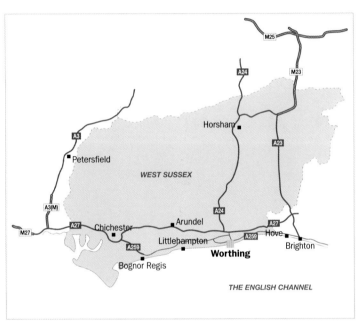

You'd have thought that the human race would've taken heed of what happened to Icarus. But no. The human spirit yearns to take flight, and so the International Birdman launches competitors off Worthing Pier every year to prove what we all know deep down in our hearts to be true. Birds can fly. We can't.

It's a flight of fancy to think that humans can stay airborne for more than a few seconds before gravity puts its weighty foot down. But that's never stopped us from trying. Ever since Icarus proved it takes more than wax and feathers, we've been itching to master the power of flight.

Well, here's your chance to shine. The Worthing International Birdman competition pits some of the brightest minds in aviation against some birdbrains, in a bid to fly the furthest from the pier. And the prize, for once, is no small beer either. For anyone who can fly for 100 metres, or more, there's a whopping £30,000 on offer. For those with more modest ambitions, like not drowning, there are prizes from £500 down to £100 in the various classes you can enter. And while the £30,000 for a 100-metre flight is usually safe, there's also a prize for the longest time in the air – irrespective of distance – £30 for every second aloft, going up to a maximum of £750.

First up is the Leonardo da Vinci class. Leo was fascinated by flight and, though his ingenuity outstripped the technology of 16th-century Italy, he left designs for various flying machines,

❝ ...IT'S PRETTY SUICIDAL IF
YOU'RE IN THE FUN-FLIERS'
CLASS AND AS AIRWORTHY
AS A DAIRY COW. ❞

which even included a prototype helicopter. What he would have made of the Birdman is anyone's guess, but in true da Vinci tradition, the class that bears his name is open to home-made and home-designed craft.

Next up is the Condor class, which is for modified hang-gliders and, finally, there are the Kingfisher and Corporate classes, which are for the equivalent of a marathon's fun runners: the fancy dressers, the no-hopers and the downright mad.

Now, it takes a bit of bottle to do this because it's a long drop from the pier into the sea. It's fine if you're piloting something vaguely aerodynamic that'll glide you gently down, but it's pretty suicidal if you're in the fun-fliers' class and as airworthy as a dairy cow. Because there's one small calculation worth bearing in mind when you're standing on the edge of the pier in a home-made

The Low Down

ENTRY
Anyone over 18, who can swim at least 50 metres unassisted can enter. Entry fee for one person is £50, two people £75. Application forms are available online but entries close about 4 months prior to the event and numbers are limited, so get in quick.

PRIZES
Trophies and cash prizes.

FURTHER INFO
Flying starts around 12:30pm on Saturday, 1pm on Sunday. Organisers: 01903 203252; www.worthingbirdman.co.uk.

sequinned jumpsuit and a handful of pink ostrich feathers: the free-falling human body accelerates at 32 feet per second, every second, up to a terminal velocity of around 120 miles per hour ($v(t) = -gt + v0$ if you're at all technically inclined, or not just willing to accept that it's fast and scary).

Each Leonardo and Condor class aviator gets two flights, one on Saturday and one on Sunday if your craft and/or your bottle remain intact, and points are awarded for the distances covered. For the majority of aviators, though, the only prize they're likely to win is the

People's Choice Award, which goes to the favourite Kingfisher class nutter who gets £100 to put towards the cost of their personal injury insurance. Because, while quite a few folk take part in the Worthing International Birdman on a wing and a prayer, most of them have neither.

World Bog Snorkelling Championships

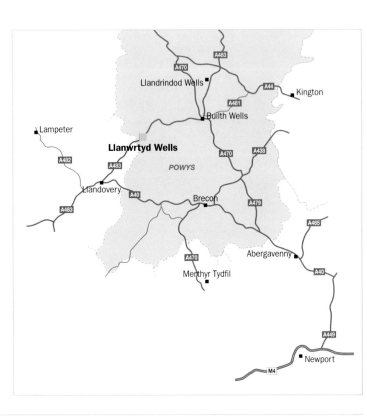

This is possibly not the best place to use flippers and a snorkel, but is probably the brightest thing you can do with 60 yards of Welsh bog...Unless, of course, you like snorkelling on mountain bikes, in which case the World Bog Snorkelling Championships' crazy biking cousin is the event for you (see p94).

The brightest brains in tourist offices up and down the land must be scratching their heads at this one. There they are, trying to dream up campaigns to bring in the tourists with ads full of sun hats and ice creams and kids building sandcastles on the beach when two Llanwrtyd

locals go and come up with the idea of bog snorkelling over a couple of pints in the pub. And, hey presto, people are arriving in droves from all over the globe to snorkel in their bog.

The World Bog Snorkelling Championships have been running for over 20 years now

and, although Olympic status remains pending, the contest has an established place on the wacky races calendar. More than 150 competitors take part from as far abog as the US and New Zealand.

The idea is to complete two lengths of a 60-yard trench

filled with the dark and brown. You are not allowed to use any officially recognised swimming stroke, and you can only raise your head from the water for the purposes of orientation or to mouth an expletive. So, the standard stroke is the boggy paddle, a form of the doggy

paddle specially adapted for the unique conditions of a Welsh bog. You can't pretend this is sane, so it's best to enter into the spirit of the event.

So what's it like? Well, you're expecting the cold and the mud, obviously, and the lack of visibility is no surprise. The leeches can be a bit of a shock, though. Then there's the feel of a slinky eel coiling itself around your legs. And who knows what else lurks in the depths of the bog? Water scorpions occasionally put in an appearance, but supposed sightings of a giant 12-tentacled squid answering to the name of Daffyd have never actually been confirmed.

The best advice is to wear a wetsuit and a decent pair of flippers (no monofins allowed), and keep your fingers crossed it's not lunchtime for the boglife. Make sure your mask doesn't leak muddy water, too, because

❝ ...SUPPOSED SIGHTINGS OF A GIANT 12-TENTACLED SQUID ANSWERING TO THE NAME OF DAFFYD HAVE NEVER ACTUALLY BEEN CONFIRMED. ❞

The Low Down

ENTRY
Anyone over 14 can enter on the day, or pre-register via the website (recommended). Under-18s must be accompanied by an adult. Entry fee £15. Small parking donation.

PRIZES
Trophies are awarded to the winners of each category: fastest male, female, junior, local, local junior, and best fancy dress. Additional prizes for runners-up.

FURTHER INFO
Starts 11am. Organisers: 01591 610236 (The Neuadd Arms Hotel); www.green-events.co.uk.

it's hard enough as it is without being blinded by smelly bog. As for the rest, it's just a test of grit, determination and, ultimately, speed. After all, the faster you do it, the faster you'll be in the nearby stream washing the muck off. There's a minimum entry age of 14, but no maximum age (so go on Gran, give it a go) and there are fancy dress competitions for those who aren't looking to challenge the world record. Should you be crazy enough to try to break it, it's just over 1 minute 30 seconds, though a time of between two and four minutes is more bog standard.

If the bog appeals but your doggy paddle's not quite up to scratch, or if you're a keen cyclist, then you can always try the World Mountain Bike Bog Snorkelling Championships (p94), which are a pedal-power version of the same thing, though just as mad and pointless.

Football in the River

Bourton-on-the-Water seems like an appropriate place to stage a river football match, and this cross between six-a-side soccer and a nice paddle with your trousers rolled up is an annual fixture dating back over 100 years. Played between two bridges in the River Windrush, it's wet and wild, and a whole lot of fun.

Football is the global game, the one sport that unites the whole planet. Whether in South American shanty towns, African villages, the playing fields of Britain or the wastes of Siberia: you name it, football will be played there. Even the Americans play it, so it must be good.

Playing soccer in water, however, is less widespread. Of course, it's not unknown in the more northerly parts of Britain, where mid-winter matches can get a bit splashy and pitches can end up under water. But Football in the River at Bourton-on-the-Water is more deliberately wet because it takes place between bridges in the middle of the Windrush river.

Imagine if every sport were played in water. You could have snorkel snooker and water golf, tiddlysinks and, of course, just plain old pool.

Luckily, as the river passes through the ridiculously pretty little town of Bourton, it's channelled between stone embankments and under low bridges, and is only about 10 inches deep, just enough to cover the shins.

The water moves with all the speed of a big fat goalie, so doesn't really give either side

an advantage when they're kicking towards the flow.

There's a ref in traditional black kit overseeing the proverbial game of two (15-minute-long) halves. The six-a-side teams are comprised of players from local footie side Bourton Rovers, and their task is to try to score in the goals, which are placed near to the arches of the two bridges. There's never really any danger of the floodgates opening when it comes to goals; the games are usually reasonably low scoring as it's a skill and a half managing to kick the ball, let alone getting it to the right player on the right team.

It's all pretty frantic, with both teams splashing about after the ball. And if you've never tried running in shin-deep water then you won't appreciate how tiring it is. Nor will you know how much skill it takes to kick a ball that's bobbing about in the brook. Tactics are fairly rudimentary:

The Low Down

ENTRY
Only members of Bourton Rovers Football Club can play in the match, but spectators can watch the game from either side of the river bank and bridges for free.

PRIZES
No prizes, it's all about the fun.

FURTHER INFO
Kick off is at 4pm, and the village holds a fête from 11am. Waterproofs are advisable if you plan to watch the match from the river bank. Tourist Info: 01451 820211; www.bourtoninfo.com.

...BRING SOMETHING WATERPROOF, BECAUSE SEVERAL GALLONS OF THE PITCH TEND TO END UP IN THE FRONT FEW ROWS... "

aim, kick out and hope for the best, which is a whole lot funnier to watch than real football.

Grass footballers often complain about the mythical 'bobble' of an uneven pitch, but here there's just no telling where the ball's going to go, and you have to try to figure it out while wiping water from your eyes. Yellow cards for foul play are not uncommon, and are often met with a splash of water in the face for the ref. So much for the Respect Agenda trying to make footballers treat referees with a bit more civility.

A worthwhile tip for budding spectators is to bring something waterproof, because several gallons of the pitch tend to end up in the front few rows as players splash their way through the game and stop for the occasional water fight. But it's a small price to pay to witness one of the funniest of the mad adventures that make up a British summer.

World Gravy Wrestling Championships

WHO?
Gravy guzzlers and grappling fans.

WHEN?
August Bank Holiday Monday.

WHERE?
Rose 'n' Bowl pub, Newchurch Road, Stacksteads, Lancashire.

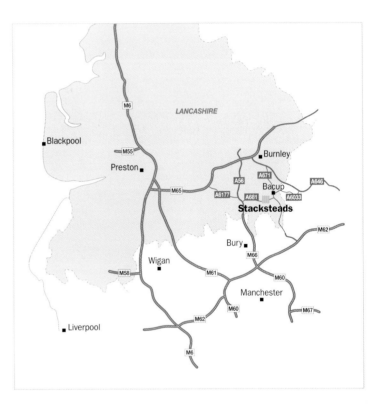

Normally something you'd expect to find on a late-night satellite channel, gravy wrestling has become respectable and is now considered a serious sport. As if. This is mucking around in a giant paddling pool. But, as Austin Powers would say, 'It's graavy baby'.

If snorkelling in a Welsh bog (see p138) doesn't wet your whistle, maybe this will float your gravy boat.

In a 16-feet paddling pool in Lancashire, grapplers come together every year to wrestle each other in two inches of real gravy. Everything you'd expect to

see at a WWF wrestling match is here: the moves, the throws, the costumes and the characters. And just like in WWF, it's really more for comic effect than as a serious sport, despite the half-nelsons and headlocks.

Adhering to the regular rules of wrestling, there are points on offer for fighting performance and the execution of various technical moves, like a Take Down, where you wrestle your opponent into the gravy and hold them there. Getting out of a Take Down is an Escape and then there's a Reversal (you reverse a Take Down, Escape and take your opponent down to gravy level yourself). As in real wrestling, a Fall is when you hold your opponent's shoulders down in the brown for a count of three.

But the heaviest scoring is for the fun factor, such as the contestant who receives the loudest applause, who's got the

best costume and, not something you'd want to try with Hulk Hogan, who gets the biggest laugh.

You can even gift points to your opponent by such infringements as aggression, roughness and unsportsmanlike conduct. And just so you're in no doubt, this is a family show, so anyone who comes along expecting to see babes in bikinis will get quite a shock as Five-Bellies Bill and Frank the Tank take to the Bisto.

To keep things interesting, buckets of gravy are also thrown at the wrestlers during the bout and, if competitors flag, the referee is likely to shove them back together smartish and tell them to get on with it.

It might all sound like serious fun, but for two small technical details. First, the gravy, though real, is past its sell-by date. So it's a little tangy and you don't want to be swallowing too much of it. Second, it isn't warm

...ANYONE WHO COMES ALONG EXPECTING TO SEE BABES IN BIKINIS WILL GET QUITE A SHOCK AS FIVE-BELLIES BILL AND FRANK THE TANK TAKE TO THE BISTO. "

and gooey. This gravy is stone cold. But none of this deters competitors, who compete in the men's and women's singles events, and the new sportsmen category, which is designed for people with a more serious interest in wrestling (ie folk who aren't just there for a laugh).

The judges try to pair opponents on the basis of height and weight, but it's all rather approximate, so you might find yourself stepping into the pool with someone you'd never invite round for dinner. And because it's a straight knockout competition, with the winner of

each round progressing, you could end up with someone really tasty in the final.

But then again, it could be just your luck to step into the ring to face Frank the Tank with a hungry look in his eye.

Brambles Bank Cricket Match

WHO?
Anyone called Sandy.

WHEN?
Late August/early September depending on the tide.

WHERE?
Brambles Sandbank, the Solent.

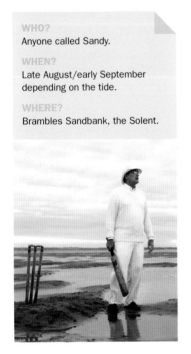

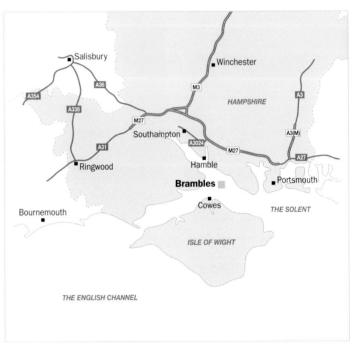

What could be more evocative of a British summer than a cricket match? White flannels flapping in the breeze, gentle swing bowling, the odd cry of 'Howzat?' and applause for a well-hit boundary. And sand. And puddles. And having to get back to the pavilion by motor launch. Yes, it's tidal cricket on the sands of the Solent.

The Brambles Sandbank out in the middle of the Solent is halfway between Southampton and the Isle of Wight, and only pokes its head above the sea once a year, when the tide is at its lowest. And what more spiffing way to celebrate the appearance of this part-time island than to

row out to it and stage a cricket match on the bumpy sands?

Even before the advent of the shortened form of the great game, like one-day internationals and Twenty20 cricket, there was the Brambles Bank Cricket Match. The contest only lasts for an hour or so before the sea stops play and the teams have to retire to the pavilion by motor launch. The members of the Royal Southern Yacht Club in Hamble (on the mainland) and the players from the Island Sailing Club in Cowes (on the Isle of Wight) retire together for a slap-up meal and agree to make it a date again next year at the annual low tide, even if, as sometimes happens, it means the match has to be played at dawn.

Conditions, of course, are far from ideal and not a patch on the pitch at Lord's or Trent Bridge. There's no opportunity to roll the wicket and the outfield is always

❝ THE SANDBANK IS IN FACT A SHIPPING HAZARD
(THE QE2 RAN AGROUND ON IT IN 2007)... ❞

a little on the damp side; that's when it's not pockmarked with salty puddles. And the bounce is unpredictable, so batsmen often advance from the crease to take the full toss. Having a fielder at short leg tends to be a good idea, because the ground's uneven and there's usually more than one

fielder who ends up looking like a silly mid-on.

The teams take it in turns to win the match, because there's not really much point in trying to get competitive on a pitch that won't take spin, and whose boundaries are the advancing waves. As a result, tactics deviate a little

from the grass-based version of the game. Restraining a batsman from making a shot is not uncommon. Tripping or rugby tackling the batsmen running between the wickets is an easy way to save runs, and while the full toss at least gives the batsman a chance of hitting the

The Low Down

ENTRY
Teams consist of members of the two sailing clubs. Open to any spectators, but they need to arrange a ride with one of the clubs, or have their own boat.

PRIZES
No prizes, it's all about the fun.

FURTHER INFO
Start time depends on the tide. Organisers: the Island Sailing Club in Cowes – 01983 296621; www.islandsc.org.uk or the Royal Southern Yacht Club in Hamble – 02380 450300; www.royal-southern.co.uk.

ball, there's nothing like trying to dig a sandy Yorker out from beneath your feet to make you realise this isn't easy.

The game dates back to the 1950s and was first played, bizarre though it may sound, between the inmates of Pankhurst Prison and their wardens. At least there was little chance of any of the prisoners absconding.

The sandbank is in fact a shipping hazard (the QE2 ran aground on it in 2007), especially when passing skippers are disturbed by the vision of cricketers seemingly playing atop the water.

The bank is shifting around the channel as the tide drags the sand slowly westward. So, it's worth grabbing the chance to see 22 men and their supporters standing in the middle of the Solent on a fine summer's morning before the pitch ends up under the waves forever.

Autumn

The Great British Duck Race

A quarter of a million plastic ducks racing down the Thames isn't something you see every day. Nor is a first prize of £10,000 for the winning duckie and its sponsor, which makes the Great British Duck Race on the upper Thames, near Hampton Court Palace, the most lucrative duck race in the world. Probably.

This annual charity event, which began in 2006 and has fast become a permanent fixture on Britain's summer sporting calendar, sees hundreds of thousands of individually sponsored plastic ducks in a lazy race down a slow stretch of the River Thames by Hampton

Court Palace. It is, along with the Oxford and Cambridge Boat Race, one of the very rare occasions when the river is closed to traffic.

The ducks are set afloat in Molesey Lock, and can be seen jostling for a good position near the starting gates just like the horses before the Grand National begins. But at the off there's no mad scramble. The plastic creatures are penned into a channel rather than being left to float free on the Thames, and so instead of racing off downstream the ducks spread like some kind of monstrous algae bloom from a 1950s B-movie.

Depending on the tidal conditions and the fitness of the ducks, it can take a couple of hours of serious paddling for the first duck to cover the 1-kilometre course down to the finish line at the Sheriff Boat Club at Albany Reach. You'd like to think that the winner would get to

❝ ...INSTEAD OF RACING OFF DOWNSTREAM THE DUCKS SPREAD LIKE SOME KIND OF MONSTROUS ALGAE BLOOM FROM A 1950S B-MOVIE. ❞

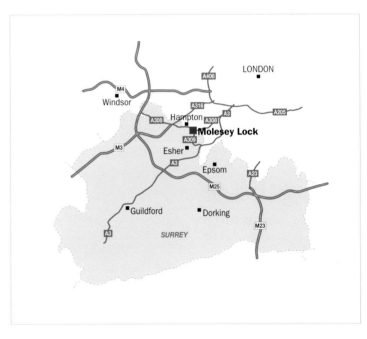

WHO?
Anyone who gives a duck.

WHEN?
The Sunday after the August Bank Holiday (usually early September).

WHERE?
Molesey Lock, nr Hampton Court, Surrey.

climb the podium to attend a prize-giving ceremony in which it sprays a bottle of Hoisin sauce over itself, but there's no such luck for the winning duck. Instead these little plastic fellows are scooped up into cardboard boxes and are – whisper it, and don't tell the ducks – recycled.

It costs £2 to sponsor a duck, with all the proceeds going to charity bar the whopping £10,000 first prize and 30 other prizes for the runners-up. Sponsorship is carried out online and each month from February, when registration opens for the race itself, every duck that's already

been sponsored is entered into a draw for a monthly cash prize. So there's quite an incentive to get in there early for the choicest ducks and start their training.

Surprisingly perhaps, for a race with an average speed of about half a mile an hour, the banks of the Thames are lined with

spectators cheering on their racers. Not that anyone can tell which duck's which, because they're all identical, and it's only when the winning duck is plucked from the water that anyone will know his or her identity. Still, it's the taking part that counts, and it's all for a good cause. The aim is to raise £500,000 for charity, and each year the organisers look to beat their own world record for the number of ducks raced. Let Brazil keep winning the World Cup, let the All Blacks be the best at rugby, let the Yanks whip our asses in the Ryder Cup. As long as we're still setting world records for the greatest number of simultaneously floating plastic ducks on a stretch of navigable river, we, as a nation, can hold our heads up high.

So, never let it be said that the great British public don't give a duck. Because we do. A quarter of a million of them.

Onion Eating Competition

Fayre Stewards' Stall
and Information

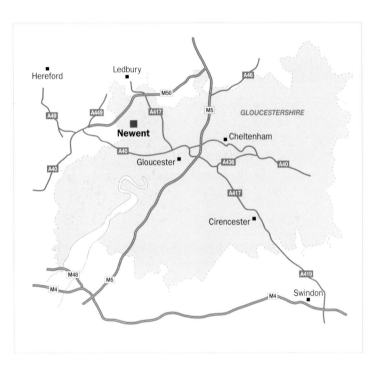

Normally you'd need a hypnotist to convince you that the raw onion you're eating is really an apple before you would even dream of entering this contest. But some folk will do anything for a small silver trophy, the adulation of a sizeable crowd and a free onion.

Every year the world's leading eaters of onions flock to the Newent Onion Fayre. It's the Wimbledon, the Wembley, the Lord's of onions. And ever since the 13th century, it has annually seen the little hosting town of Newent, nestled in the Forest of Dean, go onion mad. The reason

for the town's obsession with the onion is a little obscure, but the day-long festival is timed to coincide with the first day of the harvest, and the official version is that Welsh drovers used to pass through these parts with their cattle and liked to take home a supply of the local onions.

Nowadays, the fayre is a more general celebration of fresh produce, with stalls and shops selling all kinds of varieties of fresh fruit and veg, a shop-window competition and a prize for the kid who's made the best looking vegetable-animal. However, it's the onion that's the belle of this particular ball, and the town sells about five tons of them during the day, so it's a real onion-fest. And it's the onion eating competition that really draws in the crowds.

Now, onions are nice when they're caramelised, or pickled, or fried in olive oil with some garlic. A few

pieces of chopped-up raw onion in a salad is just about acceptable, and onion rings in batter are great. But to try to eat a whole six-ounce raw onion is a little on the obsessive side.

At least in contrast to the hour-long trial of the World Stinging Nettle Eating Championship (see p70), this is a sprint event with just a single onion to be consumed in the fastest possible time. The world record for seeing off an average-sized onion (about the size of a Granny Smith) is currently 48 seconds.

And just like the much maligned nettle, when you peel away the layers, you'll find that the onion has all sorts of medicinal properties, such as reducing the swelling from bee stings, and it is even rumoured – though please keep this to yourselves – that onion can act as an aphrodisiac. So, that's something to bear in mind and pass the time as you

The Low Down

ENTRY
Free entry for both the men's and ladies' competitions (there are 12 places in each). You can enter just prior to the contest.

PRIZES
Trophies are presented to the winners of each competition (to be held for the year and then returned for next year's contest).

FURTHER INFO
The fayre starts at 10am and the onion eating competition is at 1pm. Tourist Info: 01531 822468; or see www.newentonionfayre.org.

...ONIONS ARE NICE WHEN THEY'RE CARAMELISED, OR PICKLED, OR FRIED IN OLIVE OIL WITH SOME GARLIC... BUT TO TRY TO EAT A WHOLE SIX-OUNCE RAW ONION IS A LITTLE ON THE OBSESSIVE SIDE.

munch your way through your onion's tough and pungent flesh.

There are all sorts of old wives' tales about how to avoid onions stinging your eyes. One is to place a silver teaspoon upside down in your mouth (doesn't work). Another is to use a very sharp knife because it slices rather than crushes the onion, limiting the release of the sulphenic acid that irritates the eyes (works a bit). But the only failsafe way to avoid the sting is to chop your onion in a bowl of water, which drowns the nasty tear-inducing chemical.

But none of these are likely to help you win the competiton, as they aren't permitted, so the best idea is probably to wear ski goggles. You might look a fool, but at least you won't be crying. Or you could just avoid all the fuss and the sting completely by cramming the whole onion in your mouth and eating it that way. Anything else is just likely to end in tears.

World Black Pudding Throwing Championships

**DANGER
LOW FLYING
PUDDINGS**

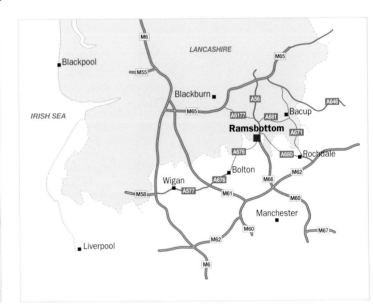

The final skirmishes of the Wars of the Roses are played out by a pub in Greater Manchester, where black puddings are thrown at a tray of Yorkshire puddings in the hope of settling an ancient rivalry. Fat chance. It's amazing just how long some folk will hold a grudge.

The 15th-century spat between the houses of Lancaster and York wasn't, as you might think, a battle between two top fashion houses to be the queen of vogue, but a full-blown war over who got to be king of the castle.

You'd think the Wars of the Roses would be history by now,

but oh no. Some folk just can't let it lie. That old rivalry between the white rose of York and the red rose of Lancaster is still alive and well in the town of Ramsbottom.

These days the Yorkists and Lancastrians are playing out their ancient grudge using nothing more dangerous than perishable pieces of a staple northern diet: black pudding.

Anyone old enough to remember 1970s comedy gods *The Goodies* will recognise the blood-curdling Lancashire martial art of Eckythump, in which novices in flat caps were fed a diet of black pudding and chip butties and were taught the art of pudding-to-pudding combat. The weapons in question, a mixture of congealed pig's blood, spices, suet and rusk wrapped in a length of intestine, looked like a robber's cosh but were really as soft as putty.

So, the World Black Pudding Throwing Championships aren't

the first to use the black pudding as a means of settling old scores, though here in Ramsbottom it's a gentler and more considered form of weaponry. But there's something not quite right about all this. As a nation we hold contests to eat things we shouldn't, like nettles and raw onions (see p70 and p160), while throwing around the stuff we should eat, like eggs (see p86) and black pudding.

Anyway, the deal here is that the proud burghers of Bury in Greater Manchester, originally from the Lancaster side of the divide, throw black pudding (red rose food) at a pile of Yorkshire puddings (white rose food). The aim is to humiliate the Yorkshire puddings, bring them down a peg or two, which is relatively easy because they're up on a 20-feet platform. It's a fairly low-scoring contest for both juniors and seniors because throwers have to launch their puddings underarm,

YOU'D THINK THE WARS OF THE ROSES WOULD BE HISTORY BY NOW, BUT OH NO. ❞

so there's a tendency for them to land on the tray of 12 Yorkshire puddings rather knocking any of them off. So it's a lot harder than it looks and a fair degree of skill is required to dislodge anything.

The black puddings are wrapped in ladies' tights, both to keep them in shape and to make them look more attractive, and are thrown by each competitor, who must keep one foot on what's known as the Golden Grid. Even though it looks like a lamé drain cover, it's obviously of symbolic importance. Like something from a Dan Brown novel, the Golden Grid is held in a secret location then escorted by train and carried with due solemnity by local army cadets to the Royal Oak pub, before being placed on the ground beneath the scaffold that holds the Yorkshire puddings.

This is one event where the proof of the pudding certainly isn't in the eating.

World Gurning Championships

Didn't your mother ever tell you that if you pull a funny face and the wind changes direction, you'll be stuck like that for ever? Obviously not. Gurning is the ancient art of pulling grotesque faces, and nowhere does it better than this small town in west Cumbria.

We've all gurned at some time or another – over a horrible taste, a nasty shock or somebody else's broken wind. Pull a funny face and things never seem so bad. Give it a try sometime.

Or come to Cumbria for the World Gurning Championships, where the ancient art of looking

unsightly for pleasure and reward has been keeping folk entertained for centuries. Competitors place their heads through a horse harness and make the most grotesque face that the elasticity of their features will allow.

The origins of gurning are gloriously unclear. It's not even certain where the word itself comes from. It could be a derivation of the Anglo-Saxon 'grin', meaning to catch in a noose or snare (perhaps a reference to the horse harness). Or it could come from the Middle English word 'girn' meaning to bear the teeth in anger.

The origins of the competition are no clearer. One story about how the annual gurning competition at Egremont began is that in 1267 the local landlord gifted a cart of crab apples to the villagers but they were so tart that when they bit into them there was a mass involuntary gurn. Another is that

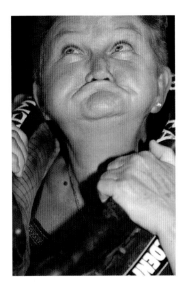

**❝ ...THE ANCIENT ART OF LOOKING UNSIGHTLY
FOR PLEASURE AND REWARD HAS BEEN
KEEPING FOLK ENTERTAINED FOR CENTURIES. ❞**

at some point in the past the village idiot used to entertain the locals with his funny faces. They'd throw a horse collar over him and, in return for a pint of ale, have him gurn for their amusement.

However it got started, it's here now, and there's no point turning your nose up at it. Well, maybe

there is. The rules of the game are simple: head through the collar, pull a funny face, everyone claps and cheers, job done.

You're not allowed to use your hands or anything else to distort your face, it all has to come from within, and you're judged on both grotesqueness and also the

extent of the transformation from your normal, everyday Clarke Kent exterior. So you can't just take off your nerdy glasses, give yourself a kiss curl and fool everyone into thinking you're Superman. It doesn't work like that.

Having false teeth is a big help, because you are allowed to take

ENTRY
Anyone can enter on the evening of the contest, with admission to the hall and entry to the gurning competition free, although donations are requested. Men's, ladies' and juniors' categories.

PRIZES
Trophies for the winners.

FURTHER INFO
Events take place around town all day. The Championsips start at 6pm. Organisers: 01946 824352 after 4:30pm then 01946 821220 after 6pm on weekdays; www.egremontcrabfair.com.

them out and this increases the chance that you can swallow your own nose (always a top party trick). Bulging eyes are good, as long as they don't come all the way out. Rubbery features, malleable lips and a general ability to look a little off kilter will also help separate you from the run-of-the-mill uglies. And it's handy to think of something startlingly unpleasant, like sitting on a wasps' nest in your birthday suit, or that you're auditioning for the part of an alien in *Doctor Who*. Grab a mirror and give it a go.

Whatever technique you adopt, just make sure that the wind doesn't change direction while you're in mid-gurn, otherwise there's a danger that you'll stay like that for ever. And while it might win you the title of men's or ladies' World Champion Gurner, what are you going to do for the other 364 days of the year?

World Conker Championships

WHO?
Nutcases.

WHEN?
The second Sunday in October.

WHERE?
New Lodge Fields, Polebrook, nr Oundle, Northamptonshire.

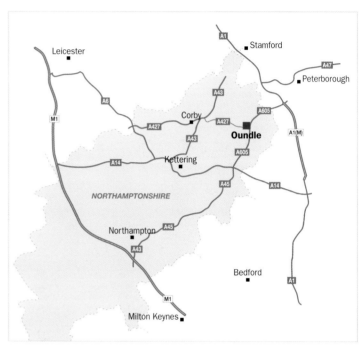

'I came, I saw, I conkered.' Every Brit's had a go at conkers at some time in their lives, and you might even think you're quite good. But the World Conker Championships are a tougher nut to crack. After all, they attract nutters from all around the world.

Another great playground favourite, the game of conkers goes back to ancient times, when Britain was covered by a vast forest and conkers (horse chestnut tree seeds) were used as currency and, long before the days of Willy Wonka, the first everlasting gobstoppers.

The game is thought to have been invented in 1848, at the height of the Victorian era, when Britain had conkered a quarter of the globe. But it wasn't until 1965 that the game was organised enough to stage the first World Conker Championships on Ashton's village green. It was something of a local affair, held in the shade of horse chestnut trees. After the event moved to Oundle it began to grow and to attract conkerers from far and wide to battle it out. The fateful year of 1976 saw the world title go overseas for the first time, to a Mexican conkistador, and both the men's and ladies' titles have since regularly been won by contestants from abroad.

The game is fairly simple. Players take it in turns to have three strikes at their opponent's nut until one or other nut smashes. Sometimes it can be the target nut, sometimes it's the attacking

> **GIVING EACH PLAYER STANDARD-ISSUE NUTS HELPS ENSURE THAT THE COMPETITION IS A TEST OF PURE SKILL AND TECHNIQUE.**

nut. In a few cases, where real hard nuts are involved, the contest can be timed out after five minutes and moves into a sort of penalty shoot-out. There's a total of nine strikes each (again three each, in turn) and, if the conkers are tough nuts to crack, the winner is the player who's scored the most clean hits and avoided snagging (that's getting the conker strings tangled).

The organisers supply all the conkers themselves. These specially prepared comp nuts are designed to prevent contestants from using an ineligible conker they've baked and soaked in vinegar themselves. Giving each player standard-issue nuts helps ensure that the competition is a test of pure skill and technique.

Now, as you can imagine, conkers can be dangerous. It is a contact sport, after all, and the aim of the game is the total obliteration of the opponent's nut. The dangers

The Low Down

ENTRY
Over-18s must apply online by
1st Oct: £10 entry fee. Under-
18s can enter on the day for £1.
Spectators: adult £4, concession
£2, family ticket £10.

PRIZES
Winners receive a trophy to keep
and have their names engraved on
a cup, which stays with the club.

FURTHER INFO
Registration and check-in
opens at 8am; play starts at
10:30am; entertainment till 3pm.
Organisers: 01293 889889; www.
worldconkerchampionships.com.

are such that in some schools, for example, head teachers have tried to ban conkers from the playground or insist that children wear goggles in case of flying shards. But, for once, the fears have been overblown.

In 2007 the World Conker Championships were actually sponsored by the Institution for Occupational Safety and Health. Okay, it was a PR exercise for the white-coat-and-clipboard brigade, who wear permanent frowns and are taught how to tut at the taxpayer's expense, but even so it's nice to see they have a sense of humour.

So, now that we're free to go forth and conker, it's time to restore some pride to the British game. Let's prove once again to all-comers and conkerers from across the globe that, when it comes to arcane sports, we remain the world's finest nutters.

World Crazy Golf Championships

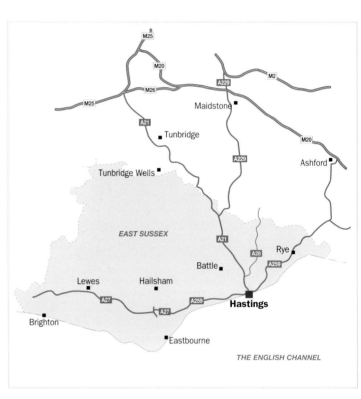

THE ENGLISH CHANNEL

Some of the worst golfers in the world compete in the World Crazy Golf Championships. Certainly they're some of the worst dressed, but what they lack in the sartorial stakes they make up for in drive. So put your money where your mouth is: grab a putter and have a flutter.

Real golf can be pretty crazy as it is. Anyone who's tried playing on a public course on a Sunday will know that some people manage to create their own obstacles by ending up in a neighbour's garden and having to bend a recovery shot between two garden gnomes and an

ornamental water feature. On the rougher courses you even have to invent your own rules, like getting a free drop when your ball ends up in the passenger seat of a burnt-out panda car abandoned on the seventh green.

Crazy golf at least makes all these challenges rational.

For a game usually associated with seaside resorts and holiday camps, played by men with rolled-up trousers and kids with sticky fingers, the World Championships afford crazy golf the stamp of a respectable sport. And it's weirdly popular too, particularly in the US, where there were once

estimated to be 30,000 courses, including 150 built on New York rooftops, and in Germany, where a whopping 15,000,000 crazies take up a mini putter every year.

Back in Blighty, and in keeping with the tradition that the Open is always held on a links course by the sea, the World Crazy Golf

Championships take place on a couple of seafront courses in Hastings, East Sussex, to allow wind and rain to spice up the contest.

Overseen by the British Minigolf Association (BMGA), the event comprises 36 holes of stroke play (that's the aggregate number of shots overall) played on two 18-hole courses with features such as mini waterwheels and windmills. Luck plays a huge part in the proceedings, but then when you consider that in the first six years of the World Championships the same man, Tim Davies, won the men's competition five times, you have to concede that skill plays its part as well.

Putting the ball over bridges, through tunnels and over undulating felt greens into the cup is quite a challenge. A perfect round in crazy golf is 18 – that's 18 holes-in-one – and is naturally as rare as hen's teeth. Top scores

The Low Down

ENTRY
Anyone over 14 can enter. £25 for 6 rounds of golf (plus British Minigolf Association membership fee of £20 for the year). Places are limited and the event is usually fully subscribed by August, so register early via the website.

PRIZES
Prize money for the top few places, around £1,000 for the winner.

FURTHER INFO
Check in 9–10:30am both days. Play starts at 10:30am. Organisers: 01424 437227; or see www.minigolf.org.uk.

are usually in the 30s, with the course record a crazy 31.

To add to the confusion, there's a host of different balls to use. Unlike real-world golf, where the white dimpled ball is standard, crazy golf allows contestants to select a ball from a range with all sorts of different properties, such as size, weight, bounce, hardness and, most important of all to the fashion-conscious crazy golfer, colour. So, you might choose a 42-gram rough blue bulldog with a 36-centimetre bounce, for example, when conditions are just so, but change to a 38-millimetre lacquered red bulldog with a 27-centimetre bounce when the wind's up. It's all part of the skill of the game.

The putters have a rubberised face for greater touch and feel, too, so no golfer can blame his or her clubs when things don't quite go to plan.

National Singles Tiddlywinks Championship

WHO?
Serious winkers.

WHEN?
A weekend in early October.

WHERE?
Selwyn Diamond, Selwyn College, Cambridge University, Cambridgeshire.

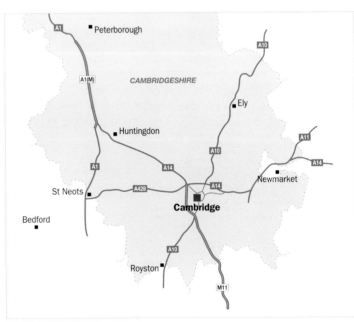

And you thought tiddlywinks was just for kids. This is a serious game, almost a sport, and it's where serious winkers come to show off their tiddlies. The winner of the English National Singles Title wins the right to challenge for the world crown, so get your squidgers at the ready.

What's the difference between a sport and a game? The answer is beer. You can't drink beer during a proper sport, but you can during a game. So, snooker and darts used to be games, back in the days when the players swilled pints throughout the match, but both have graduated to sports

because players now sip mineral water instead. The next logical step in their evolution into serious sports will be isotonic drinks and energy bars.

So, what does this mean for tiddlywinks? Well, it's a game. It's still on the first rung of the competitive ladder. You can drink beer while playing it and, until some winker turns up with a bottle of mineral water, it'll stay that way. That doesn't mean it can't be cut-throat competitive, though. After all, the English National Singles Title is at stake, and you don't win that on a simple nod and a wink.

The championship is overseen by the ETwA (English Tiddlywinks Association), set up in the mid-1950s when the modern game came into being, although tiddlywinks is actually a late Victorian invention. The first tiddlywink patent was filed by one Joseph Fincher of Oxford Street

in 1888. Imagine the excitement patent clerks must have felt in reading, by gaslight, patent application number 16,215: 'A new and improved game played with two sets of counters of different sizes and a bowl made of china or some other substance, or small pieces of wood, counters, and a bowl, the object of the pieces of wood, or of the larger counters being to press the edge of the smaller counters and cause them to jump into the bowl.'

It gives you a tingle just reading it.

In case the patent wasn't clear, the basic idea of the game is to use your squidger to squoop and gromp your winks into the pot, blitzing and bombing if necessary Got it? No? Okay, first some technical terms.

The ETwA produces a glossary to help the novice winker tell his squidger from his pot. The squidger is the small round disc

...THE BASIC IDEA OF THE GAME IS TO USE YOUR SQUIDGER TO SQUOP AND GROMP YOUR WINKS INTO THE POT, BLITZING AND BOMBING IF NECESSARY. "

used to propel the little winks into the pot, which sits in the middle of a 6 x 3-feet mat. So far so good. The varieties of shot include the squoop (playing a wink so it rests on another wink), the knock-off (a reverse squoop), the Carnovsky (a successful pot from the baseline) and the gromp

(jumping over a pile of winks on to another wink). Tiddlies (points) are scored for successful pots and for covering the other player's winks, rendering them unplayable. The game is limited to 20 minutes and the winner is the player with the greatest accumulated score by the end.

Over the tournament scores are aggregated so winning margins are as important as outright wins.

Joseph Fincher, by the way, was a man of endless invention and also filed patents for double-sleeve cufflinks and an improvement for candlestick design. He was no one-wink wonder.

Carrying the Flaming Tar Barrels

WHO?
Broad-shouldered pyromaniacs.

WHEN?
Bonfire Night (5th November).

WHERE?
The town centre, Ottery St Mary, Devon.

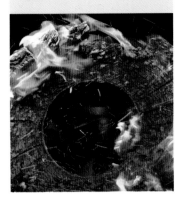

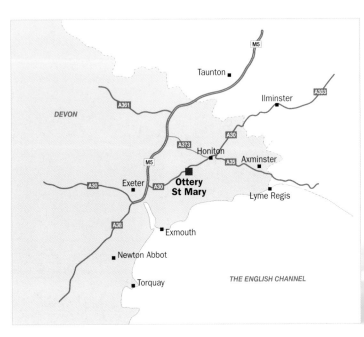

Come and watch men, women and children carrying blazing tar barrels, for no apparent reason, through the dark streets of a small Devon town. Held each year on Bonfire Night, the ritual's origins may be unclear, but it makes for a spectacular alternative to holding a sparkler and watching a wet bonfire fizzle.

In a country where suings are rife, it's good to know that there are some places left where the words 'at your own risk' still mean something. And there aren't too many more risky things you can do on Bonfire Night than hoist a 30-kilogram barrel of burning tar on to your back and go haring

around town trailing sparks and bits of blazing wood in your wake.

This is one of the few events that isn't a gimmick or tourist trick, or something dreamed up over a few pints down the local in 1974. Instead it's a genuine relic of an age-old tradition. It's thought to have begun in the 17th century; some suggest an actual date: 1688, the year of the Glorious Revolution when Dutch Protestant William III replaced Catholic King James II on the British throne, and began the age of constitutional monarchy.

How it came to take place on the 5th November, and exactly what connection, if any, there is to Guy Fawkes is unclear. Certainly the town builds a 30-feet tall bonfire and tops it off with a traditional Guy, but that may be a later addition because there are various theories as to the origin of the event. The barrels may have been used to fumigate shops, or

they may have their roots even further back in time, as part of long-lost pagan fire rituals. Some say the fire is designed to purge the streets of evil spirits.

Any which way, running the tar barrels (known locally as 'rolling') has become a communal centrepiece for the townsfolk of

Ottery St Mary, who guard the event jealously, making sure that no one interferes with it or changes its traditions.

There are 17 barrels in all, each sponsored by a local pub (you just knew there'd be beer involved) and each is lit outside its sponsoring pub, most of

which are in or close to 'the Square' on Mill Street and Yonder Street. In keeping with tradition, a succession of people, often generations of the same family, carry the barrels. Wearing hessian-sack mittens to protect them from the flames, each roller hands on to the next until the heat

THE WHOLE EVENT MAKES FOR A THRILLING, NOISY AND ADRENALINE-FUELLED SPECTACLE FOR THE CROWD... ❞

becomes too much to bear or the barrel starts to break and to carry on would burn holes in your hair, then it's time for the next barrel.

Kick off is at 4pm, when the kids take to the streets, and through the afternoon and evening, as the teens and ladies roll out their barrels, the burdens get larger and heavier. At 6:30pm the bonfire is lit on the banks of the River Otter and the bigger barrels appear for the men around 8pm, carried one after another until midnight, by which time they weigh at least 30 kilograms.

The whole event makes for a thrilling, noisy and adrenaline-fuelled spectacle for the crowd members, who can feel the heat of the barrels as they pass and have to dodge the occasional shower of sparks. So, if you're planning on joining them, leave your designer gear at home and dig out that horrid sweater Auntie Hester sent you last Christmas.

Mince Pie Eating Championship

WHO?
Gluttons.

WHEN?
Late October/early November.

WHERE?
Wookey Hole Caves, Wookey Hole,
nr Wells, Somerset.

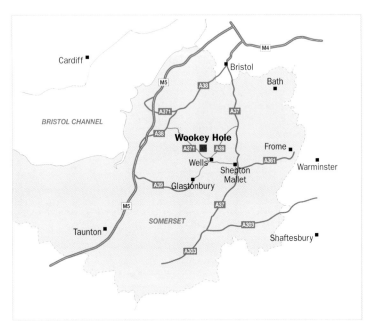

'I love a mince pie. Could eat them by the dozen.' Oh yeah? The Wookey Hole Big Eat Mince Pie Eating Championship is a large enough mouthful as it is, but come and have a go if you think you're lard enough.

How many mince pies could you eat in 10 minutes? Be honest. A six pack? Nine, perhaps? A baker's dozen? The family-sized value pack with 33 per cent extra free? Well, come to the Mince Pie Eating Championship at the Wookey Hole Big Eat and find out. There's a top prize of

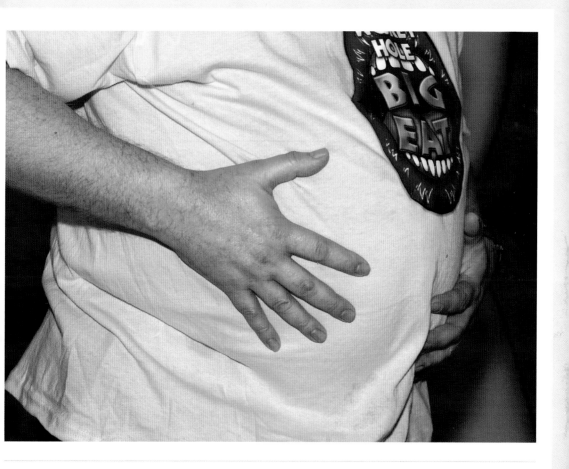

£1,000 for the most ravenous competitor, so it's worth having a think about it.

But before you pop out to the corner store for a few packets of Mr Kipling's finest, just bear this in mind: the record, set in 2006 by an American lady called Sonya Thomas, is a stomach-stretching 46 mince pies. That's a pie every 13 seconds for a full 10 minutes.

Sonya Thomas is a professional eater who has also, just for the record, downed 80 chicken nuggets in 5 minutes, 44 Maine lobsters from the shell in 12 minutes and 65 hard-boiled eggs in 6 minutes 40 seconds.

That's no yoke. And she's not your stereotypical compulsive eater in a size 20 tent-dress, either. She's a slip of a lady who doesn't look like she's got room in there for more than a few celery sticks.

However, Sonya and others like her are known as gurgitators

" THE EASY BIT IS CRAMMING THE MOUTH FULL OF PIE. ANYONE CAN DO THAT BIT. BUT THE HARD PART IS SWALLOWING IT. "

to distinguish them from mere amateurs who, after so many mince pies, are more likely to be regurgitators. A pro never heaves. It's part of the training. What goes down, stays down.

Unsurprisingly, competitive speed eating is big in the States. It's why they call it fast food. And as you can imagine, in the land of the supersized bucket meal the competition can be fierce. There's even an International Federation of Competitive Eating to oversee the speed gluttony. You can speed-eat ribs, meatballs, grits, garlicky greens, jalapeños – you name it, someone somewhere's speed-eating it. So why not mince pies? It's a shame that they're traditionally thought of as Yuletide food, as they are versatile pies with many applications. A mince pie should really be for life, not just for Christmas.

The Wookey Hole Big Eat Championship is a pro-am

The Low Down

ENTRY
Open to anyone over 18.
Admission to the venue and
entry into the competition is free.
Applications accepted online
from around July/August.

PRIZES
1st place £1,000; 2nd place
£100; 3rd place £50.

FURTHER INFO
The competition starts at midday.
NOTE: This event may take a
break in 2010, but will be back
on in 2011. Organisers: 01749
672243; www.wookey.co.uk.

guzzle-fest with only 12 places around the table, some for pro gurgitators and some for hungry amateurs keen to test their mettle against the fastest gluttons in the west.

The pies are of the traditional Christmas variety, and technique is key. The easy bit is cramming the mouth full of pie. Anyone can do that bit. But the hard part is swallowing it. Without getting into the intricacies of mastication or the production of saliva, it can be pretty difficult to get the pies down after a while. So a slow and steady approach with regular gulps of water is the way to an unhealthy total. And cheating is not an option people – this is serious stuff – anyone caught dropping a pie down a sleeve is out. Any total over 20 pies is pretty good going, but you'd have to be more than a little peckish and have a stomach like a bin bag to get much further.

Winter

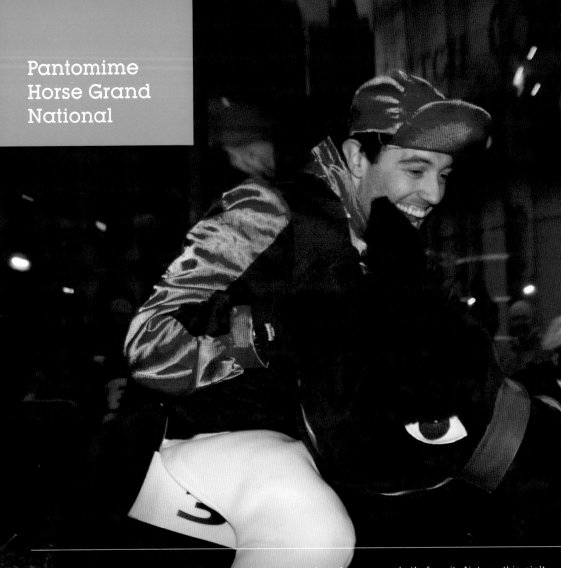

Pantomime Horse Grand National

Famous far and wide, this is the premier pantomime horse race in the world. With separate runnings for colts and fillies, the event offers all the thrills and spills of the real thing, raced around a testing 2-furlongs-long course with 12 hay-bale hurdles to jump.

Let's face it. Aintree, this ain't. It doesn't have anything like the same cachet. It doesn't attract Middle Eastern oil sheikhs in helicopters, or Russian oligarchs in blacked-out limos. There are no multi-million pound flutters on a favourite mount. And there are no on-course bookies in pork-pie

hats and suede carcoats rubbing their hands at the prospect of the year's biggest pay day.

But the Pantomime Horse Grand National, run on a course around Centenary Square in Birmingham, is every bit as much of a horse race as the real thing. Well, without the horses, obviously.

And with 2-feet-high hay bales instead of 6-feet-high fences like Becher's Brook and the Chair. And the 'horses' are two legs short of a standard stallion. They're not the two-person pantomime horses with one playing the head and the other breaking their back at the rear

end. These things are one-person horses, if that makes any sense.

But apart from that, it's all there. The 40-or-so jockeys are decked out in their traditional silks and crowds line the course. The competitors parade through the paddock to show off their steeds, with names such as

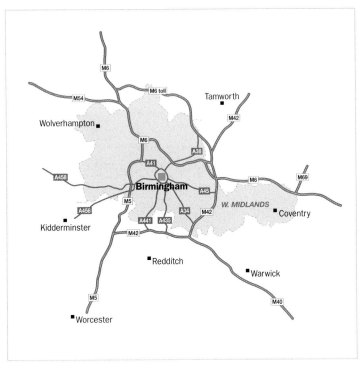

WHO?
Two-legged colts and fillies.

WHEN?
A Sunday in late November/
early December.

WHERE?
Hyatt Hotel, Centenary Square,
Birmingham, West Midlands.

Neigh Chance and Why The Long Face, as the latest odds (you can actually place a bet through Tote) are bandied about. And at the off there's a mad scramble for prime position before the first fence, where inevitably there are fallers.

One thing you'll never see at the Pantomime Horse Grand National,

though, is a loose horse that's unseated its rider and is just cantering along for the hell of it. Without going into the specifics of the relationship between a pantomime horse and its rider, suffice to say that they're inseparable, other than in the most tragic of circumstances.

Admittedly, some of the racers should have long ago been put out to grass, and others are obviously on the way to the knacker's yard. Luckily for them it's a short race, but there are 12 hay-bale jumps to negotiate, as well as a chicane and a bit of gradient up the final straight.

In classic panto fashion, when the chasing pack bears down on the front-runner, the crowd shouts 'They're behind you!', the leader says, 'Oh no they aren't!', 'Oh yes they are!'. How long will this go on? Thankfully not furlong.

As is traditional in the Grand National, the riders go through the fences almost as much as they go over them, so after the ladies' race there's a bit of remedial work required to re-bale the hay and rebuild the fences for the men's race.

The Pantomine Horse Grand National was first run in 2003, so doesn't have quite the pedigree of the real thing. But it raises money for the Lord Mayor's Charity Appeal, and includes a fancy dress competition for the kiddies (at least those between 5 and 12 years-old).

And if you can't make it to Aintree to see the real four-legged thing, this is at least half as good.

London Santa Run

Christmas wouldn't be Christmas without Santa Claus. But it's no wonder children grow up confused when they see 2,000 slim and fit Santas dashing through Battersea Park in the run-up to the big day. Would the real Father Christmas please stand up? And why's he running anyway? What are reindeer for?

Santa Claus likes to keep himself in shape and pretty fit during the 364 days of the year that he's holed up in Lapland. He passes the time with a military exercise regime of present-wrapping, chimney-climbing and sleigh rides, because there's not much else to do. But as the festive

season approaches his training needs to step up a gear and it's time to get some competitions under his enormous belt.

So, every year he travels to London and warms up for the big event by taking part – incognito of course – in the London Santa Run. With all the other competitors in traditional red garb, he blends right in and can mingle anonymously in the crowd, spying out who's been good and who's been bad and who's not going to be on his Christmas card list this year.

The run takes place over two laps of Battersea Park, on the south bank of the River Thames. Appropriately for a winter race, all the proceeds go to a charity called Disability Snowsport, which, as the name suggests, raises money to make winter sports activities open to all.

The event attracts around 2,000 Santa lookalikes, some of whom

look more like the real deal than others. To be honest, most of the runners look like Santa would do after a year on an Atkins diet of reindeer steak and snowballs. Others don't do the Santa thing at all and come as elves or snowmen, which doesn't seem to be in the spirit of a Santa race, but hey ho. These days Santa probably outsources the bulk of his work to low-cost elves in far flung countries, and even his reindeer are leased. No doubt he's using Parcelforce for some of his deliveries, too.

In comparison with the global marathon Santa will have to tackle in a few weeks' time, the Battersea race is a sprint. The course is about 6 kilometres long, so it's only a 20- to 30-minute run for the fitter Santas, but over an hour for those of a more traditional Santa build. And if you did fancy trying to pick the real Santa out from the crowd, then

IN COMPARISON WITH THE GLOBAL MARATHON SANTA WILL HAVE TO TACKLE IN A FEW WEEKS' TIME, THE BATTERSEA RACE IS A SPRINT. "

he's probably more likely to be lurking somewhere at the back. For all his bluster about a fitness regime, he's still pretty lardy and, let's face it, on Christmas Eve he gets to sit back while Rudolf and his chums do all the hard work.

But if you can pick him out from the identikit crowd, you could always sidle up to him and have a quiet word in his ear about the Take That CD you'd like, or the box set of *The Vicar of Dibley*, or whatever. Don't try to slip him a fiver, though. He has his reputation to consider, after all, and because he works with children he has to undergo regular criminal record checks, so can't afford to face a rap for Yuletide fraud, or fiddling his expenses, or anything.

After all, Christmas wouldn't be Christmas with Santa banged up in Belmarsh.

The Great Christmas Pudding Race

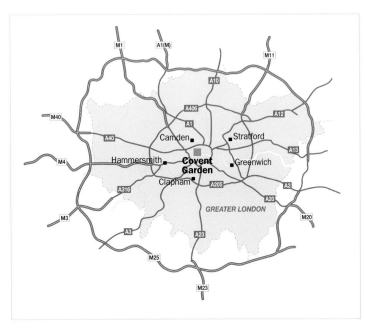

WHO?
Fruitcakes.

WHEN?
The first or second Saturday in December.

WHERE?
The West Piazza, Covent Garden, London.

The Great Christmas Pudding Race around London's Covent Garden is the perfect way to kick off the festive season. Nothing says it's Christmas more than a good old Christmas pudding with brandy cream and a sprig of holly on top.

Back in the day, when your granny made the Christmas pudding rather than buying it from M&S, it was traditional to put a sixpence in the mix. While the pudding was being made each member of the family would have a stir of the mixture and make a wish. Then whoever got

the shiny sixpence in their helping of pudding on Christmas Day was supposed to enjoy good luck for the coming year.

But the sixpence went the way of the groat and modern coins are no longer pure silver, so it's not a good idea to stick them in your pudding. A more modern alternative, to put the Chip and PIN device from a credit card into the mixture, has never really taken off. There's a danger that someone will swallow it, making future hole-in-the-wall withdrawals rather tricky affairs.

Anyway, the good old Christmas pudding forms the centrepiece of this traditional race around a specially constructed course in London's Covent Garden. Competitors in fancy dress tackle an *It's a Knockout*-style course of foam jets, inflatable slides, and balloons full of flour, while trying to keep a small pudding on a plate until they cross the finish

line. No wonder it's a popular one, given that it combines food, dressing up and running around.

Balancing your little Christmas pudding – they're of the mini dessert-for-one variety – on a tray may sound like a cinch, but the pressure to perform can get the better of some, so there's many a pud that ends up taking a tumble over the course of the race.

As they go around the route, the pudding bearers have to add stick-on facial features to their dish, so that by the end they've got a currant-and-cherry faced dessert with antler's horns of holly sprouting from its bald brown crown. Sadly, the final flourish that caps the career of any successful Christmas pudding – being doused in flammable alcohol and set alight – isn't followed here.

The competitors come along in fancy dress, usually a variety of Christmas characters from Santa

...THE PRESSURE TO PERFORM CAN GET THE BETTER OF SOME, SO THERE'S MANY A PUD THAT ENDS UP TAKING A TUMBLE OVER THE COURSE OF THE RACE. "

and Rudolph to a smattering of elves, but with the odd Smurf or Womble thrown in for good measure. There's also a bit of a trend for celebrity lookalikes. If you're impressed by that sort of thing, you might spot Her Majesty the Queen (just look out for a big hat and a handbag) or a faux Simon Cowell (the man with the Y-front Factor).

Festivities kick off with a bit of a warm up (of the competitors that is, not the puddings) before the heats get underway (just the competitors again) and then things really hot up (but not for the Christmas puds), with relay teams going head to head in the final. The prize on offer is the prestigious Christmas Pudding Trophy, but the real prize is all the money the event raises for Cancer Research UK.

Windlesham Pram Race

WHO?
Big babies and pushy parents.

WHEN?
Boxing Day (26th December).

WHERE?
Starts by the Linde Group, Chertsey Road, Windlesham, Surrey.

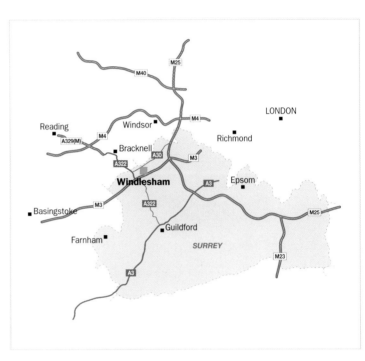

What better way to blow off the Christmas Day torpor than by racing a pram through a Surrey village on Boxing Day? But if you're feeling lazy, or just too full of Christmas pud, you could just sit back, relax and let someone else do all the pushing.

It was a privileged life when you had someone to cook for you and do all the washing up, run your bath, make your bed, tidy up after you, and so on. And whenever you fancied a turn about town, they'd wheel out a buggy, get you comfy and push you wherever you wanted to go.

Nowadays you have to win the lottery, or be in the House of Lords, to get treated like that, but back when you were a kid it just came with the territory.

The Windlesham Pram Race, a testing 3-mile push, is a chance to re-live the carefree glory days of your youth. It does include one element your mother's unlikely to have included in your childhood outings, though: the course winds it's way past all of the village watering holes and it's obligatory (for the over-18s, at least) to down half-a-pint of draught beer or a measure of spirit in each one. In essence, then, the pram race is everything you could wish for – a pub-crawl in your very own chauffeur-pushed pram (that is, if you're lucky enough to be the pushed, and not the pusher).

The event is run by the Surrey Borders Lions Club and raises money for a range of local charities and good causes.

❝ THE VEHICLES IN QUESTION ARE ONLY LOOSELY BASED ON THE CONCEPT OF A PRAM. ❞

It's been a permanent fixture on the calendar for over 40 years now, and seems to get bigger with every event. Up for grabs are prizes for the fastest pram around the course, the best looking pram and (one for all the techies out there) the best engineered pram. So if you're any good with axles and springs, that might just be the prize for you.

With the roads closed under a special provision of the Pramway Code, the event starts at 11am, which is a test in itself for those who've over-indulged on Christmas Day and are still carrying several pounds of turkey and a vat of sherry in their bellies. There's a staggered start; the serious racers set off five minutes ahead of the fun prams, which allows them to get the first round in and clear the bar before the melée begins behind them when all the fun prams turn up and start having a bit of a sesh.

The vehicles in question are only loosely based on the concept of a pram. They're not always those dinky little fold-up strollers you can take on buses, or those urban warrior pods with knobbly all-terrain tyres and disc brakes you see on the mean streets of Fulham or Chelsea, or even those old-fashioned, big-wheeled perambulators on springs that you'd expect Mary Poppins to push about. Competitors generally just take the chassis of a pram and then turn it into a *Keystone Kops*-style car, or a battleship, or something. Or they're not really anything to do with a pram at all.

In fact, some of them don't even have wheels.

One thing to bear in mind when it comes to pram design, though, is weight. Running a 3-mile course with a steel pram the size of an old Rover saloon will just give you indigestion after all the turkey and roast potatoes.

The 'Mad' Maldon Mud Race

The venue for this muddy mayhem is the primordial slime from which we came. Back in the distant past, when we were just tadpoles in shorts, this smelly stuff was home. The Malden race, through oozing mud at low tide on the Blackwater river, is one for anyone willing to muck in.

What's glorious about mud? It's uplifting as a face pack, it'll make your orchids grow strong and tall and it makes a nice home for hippos. But, when you pause to consider what's in it, you might think twice about taking a plunge into the grunge and trying to race in it. Because

when you're up to your shins in the soft and brown, and there's a stench in your nostrils like an outdoor privy, you'll realise that there are other ways to beat the post-Christmas blues.

The Maldon Mud Race is yet another pub dare. The event started in 1973, when the landlord of the local pub offered a free pint to anyone who could make it across the estuary and back at low tide. Naturally, the prospect of free beer had every mud hound donning galoshes and heading for the riverbank. The race's popularity means the days of free beer are just a memory, but the race lives on, and indeed, has gone on to prosper.

Competitors dress up in a range of strange garb. There are the fancy dressers in sumo suits, and superheroes with capes and coloured underpants. There are fun-runners in t-shirts and shorts, there are bananas,

" ...TAPE YOUR SHOES TO YOUR FEET, OR YOU'LL LOSE THEM. THIS MUD SUCKS. IN FACT, TAPING YOUR FEET TO YOUR LEGS ISN'T A BAD IDEA EITHER. "

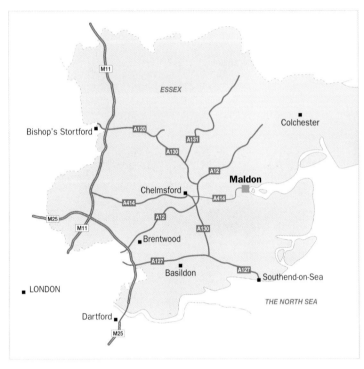

WHO?
Anyone who's 'mud' for it.

WHEN?
Late December/early January (depending on the tide).

WHERE?
Promenade Park, Maldon, Essex.

clowns and even the odd whoopie cushion or two. Mind you, after a few minutes in the mud it can be difficult to tell them all apart, because most folk soon end up negotiating the tricky terrain on their hands and knees.

The organisers, wishing to be helpful rather than put people off, make two recommendations for anyone who fancies giving it a go. First, make sure your tetanus jab is up to date. Second, tape your shoes to your feet, or you'll lose them. This mud sucks. In fact, taping your feet to your legs isn't a bad idea either. And attaching your legs securely to your torso is also recommended. You might want to get legless in the bar afterwards, but it's just not cool to lose them in the mud.

The course makes its way out into the estuary, turning right at a marker in the river then running parallel to the bank, before turning right again to head back

The Low Down

ENTRY
Entry for individuals or teams (min 4; max 6) over 18 is £25 per person online. Sponsorship money to be raised. Places are limited.

PRIZES
A medal for all who finish. Trophies for the 1st female, male and team; best male and female fancy dress; last person to complete the course, and the oldest racer. An award also goes to the person who raises the most sponsorship.

FURTHER INFO
Race starts at 11am. Organisers: www.maldonmudrace.com.

across the river to safety. It's not that far – about 400 metres in total – but even the fastest mud crawlers take about 15 minutes to complete it. And it's not just the difficulty of moving in the mud that competitors have to contend with, it's the perishing cold too. This is the middle of winter, after all. And the cold shower at the end only adds insult to injury.

Far better to watch the action unfold on the large plasma screen, a safe distance from the muck and the pong. But if you are hell-bent on trying it, the best advice is to try to stay at the front, where the mud is still smooth. If you end up following in the wake of everyone else's churned-up muck it's twice as hard to make any progress.

No wonder it took us billions of years to emerge from the primordial slime. It wasn't the slow hand of evolution at work. We were just stuck in the mud.

Mapleton Bridge Jump

Leap, feet first, into the New Year by hurling yourself, and your hangover, off a bridge into a freezing river. This splash and dash race also involves negotiating some rapids in a tiny boat, running across a field and having a nice cup of warm soup. What else do you need to see in the New Year?

As New Year resolutions go, jumping off a bridge might seem a bit extreme. Christmas wasn't that bad, was it? Okay, it was yet more socks and scented body scrub, and too much pudding and wine, but pull yourself together.

Now, jumping off bridges is not normally recommended, but in

another of those post-festivity cobweb blowers, the Mapleton Bridge Jump into the River Dove makes it all seem okay.

Contested by teams of two, the men's and women's races involve riding the river rapids in a tiny boat for a quarter of a mile or so, down to the eponymous bridge. There they hop out of the boat, climb the bridge, mount the parapet and take a deep breath (perhaps praying it won't be their last). Then they jump. If and when they resurface, they must then swim downstream for about 60 yards, before hauling themselves and their buddy out of the drink to squelch the 500 yards through a field to the finish line, where a warming cup of soup awaits. It's a doddle.

The first part of the race is usually a close-run thing. That's until competitors hit the bridge and climb the parapet. This is where the gaps can open up

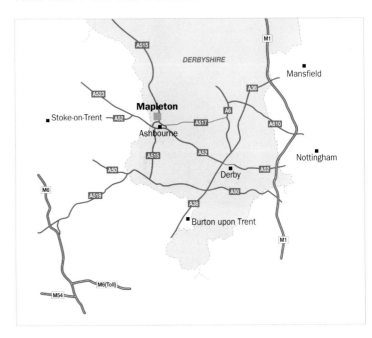

WHO?
Splashers and dashers.

WHEN?
New Year's Day (1st January).

WHERE?
Okeover Bridge, Mapleton,
nr Ashbourne, Derbyshire.

because quite a few competitors like to take their time, have a think about it and ask themselves if they really want to jump. It's only a 30-feet drop down to the river, but when you're mentally calculating the velocity of falling objects it can seem quite a bit further. The brave and the foolhardy just hurl themselves, feet first, into the river and set off on a splash and dash charge to the finish.

For top teams with no fear of heights the race takes about 15 minutes. For those with a greater regard for their own safety and well-being it can take quite a bit longer. And for some, it's a case of a bridge too far, as they don't get any further than the parapet before talking themselves back down and handing themselves over to the police.

Even if you do make it off the bridge among the front runners, there's still the cold swim to

The Low Down

ENTRY
Open to anyone over 14 and costs £5 per person. Two people per team and a max. of 20 teams in each race. Must be able to swim! Limited places so contact the organiser well in advance to enter.

PRIZES
The 'Brass Monkey' and 'Brass Iron' to the winners of the men's and ladies' races, respectively.

FURTHER INFO
The ladies' race starts at 11am, the men's at midday. Organisers: 01335 344596; www.derbyshire-peakdistrict.co.uk/mapleton.htm.

tackle and then, just when the hypothermia's making you a little light-headed and shivery, there's the home straight to run in dripping clothes and squelchy shoes. And when you finally cross the line you might find they've run out of oxtail and chicken broth, leaving just minestrone left.

The appropriately named 'Brass Monkey' trophy is on offer to the winners of the men's race, and there's a 'Brass Iron' for the ladies. Brass monkeys are supposed to be the devices used to hold cannon balls in the firing room of old ships of the line in Nelson's era. The phrase about it being cold enough to freeze the balls off a brass monkey came about because, in cold weather, the brass contracted so much that the cannon balls fell off. Or so they say. It's as good an explanation as any, and at least it doesn't involve another kind of balls.

Cold Water Swimming Championships

WHO?
Icemen and icemaidens.

WHEN?
Bi-annually (odd years), usually the fourth weekend in January.

WHERE?
Tooting Bec Lido, Tooting Common, London.

The glorious Tooting Bec Lido in London hosts this freezing plunge, and swimming caps off to anyone brave enough to dip a toe in its waters. Aficionados claim that cold water swimming brings all kinds of health benefits, but it's just as easy to visit a doctor. And a whole lot warmer.

Tooting Bec Lido has been adding a touch of Côte d'Azur glamour to south London since 1906. One of the country's oldest open-air pools, this marvel is a throwback to the days of outdoor swimming and communal baths.

The Cold Water Swimming Championships (CWSC) attract

about 300 competitors and are held every other year. Before you ask, no it's not because it takes that long to thaw out after you've competed in them. It's because they are held in between the biannual World Winter Swimming Championships, which were held here in 2008.

The Scandinavians are always big at these things. Up there they're forever sawing circular holes in the ice floe and jumping in for a relaxing dip. It's supposed to be good for you. It helps build up your immune system, improves circulation and can even give your libido a shot in the arm. In short,

cold water swimming enthusiasts claim it can give you as much of a high as, well, a few things you can buy in south London if you know where to go.

The CWSC course is a snip at 30 metres, but it's the nip in the extremities that makes it such a challenge. Worse still, the rules

stipulate that no costume may cover the arms or legs or provide any thermal protection, and you're not allowed to smear yourself in cooking oil or whale blubber or anything of that sort: it's just you and the freezing water.

Of course, jumping straight in can be dangerous. At best you hyperventilate, at worst you have a coronary, so you should get used to the cold gradually. The race is less about speed and more about resistance to the breathtaking cold. Competitors are confined to the breaststroke, as it's best not to immerse your head in the water in case your ears freeze. It also means you can wear a woolly hat. As well as medals for the fastest swimmers, there's also a special hat prize, so don't just grab any old beanie and stick it on. Give it a bit of thought and you might even win.

There are various categories open to different ages from 10 up to

ENTRY
£10 entry fee plus £5 per person for each competition entered. Relay race is £20 per team. Anyone over 10 can enter, but must be acclimatised to cold water. Enter between early November and December online. Limited places. Spectators £2.

PRIZES
Medals to the winners.

FURTHER INFO
Registration from 8am on Saturday; races start at 9am. Organisers: 020 8871 7198; www.slsc.org.uk.

80 years plus, competing either individually or in teams.

While most races are a single width of the pool, the relay is a four-person job and there's a 450-metre endurance race open just to experienced cold water swimmers, with entry by invitation only. Whichever you choose, luckily there are hot showers, a sauna and a hot tub available to help get some feeling back into your bits and bobs. But you don't want to get chilblains, so take it easy and warm back up gradually. And once you're back in your long johns and woolly tank top – who would have guessed it? – there's beer. In fact, there's a whole range of ales here, brewed originally for the 2008 World Winter Swimming Championships, with names like Chilly Willy and Blue Tits. You get the idea. And, especially for the CWSC, there's a cheeky little ale called B-B-B-Beer. B-B-B-Boom Boom.

Credits

Emma Wood is a photographer with an eye for eccentricity. Since 2006 she has been a regular at the quirkiest events in Britain, covering over 70 contests to date, but it was several rotund 8-pound Double Gloucester cheeses and a steep hill that got the idea for this book rolling. Along the way she has won the Ladies' World Mountain Bike Bog Snorkelling Championship and been runner-up in the Ladies' World Pea Shooting and Toe Wrestling Championships. She currently lives in Brighton, where she is practising her stone skimming technique.

Concept, research, photography and design by: Emma Wood
www.emmawoodphotos.com
info@emmawoodphotos.com

Written by: Keith Didcock

Publisher: Jonathan Knight

Managing Editor: Sophie Dawson

Additional research by: Cath Greenwood

Proofreaders: Leanne Bryan, Joe Roche

Marketing: Shelley Bowdler

PR: Carol Farley

Published by:
Punk Publishing Ltd, 3 The Yard,
Pegasus Place, London, SE11 5SD

Distributed by:
Portfolio Books, Suite 3/4,
Great West House, Great West Road,
Brentford, Middlesex TW8 9DF

Many of the photographs featured in this book are available for licensing. For more information, go to www.abritdifferent.co.uk.

Please note that event dates, locations and organisers' information can change, so before heading off to an event, it's advisable to double-check details on the event's website or with the local Tourist Information Office.

Punk Publishing takes its environmental responsibilities seriously. This book has been printed on paper made from renewable sources and we continue to work with our printers to reduce our overall environmental impact. Wherever possible, we recycle, eat organic food and always turn the tap off when brushing our teeth.

Emma Wood would like to thank all who grace the pages of this book, and the following supportive folk: Dave Painter, Rod Kirkpatrick, Helen Yates, Mark Sheerin, Stuart Wallace and Jason Anscomb.